THE AGE OF SELFISH ALTRUISM

Why New Values are Killing Consumerism

THE AGE OF SELFISH ALTRUISM

Why New Values are Killing Consumerism

Alan Fairnington

WILEY

John Wiley & Sons (Asia) Pte. Ltd.

Published in 2010 by John Wiley & Sons (Asia) Pte. Ltd.
2 Clementi Loop, #02–01, Singapore 129809

Other Wiley Editorial Offices
John Wiley & Sons, 111 River Street, Hoboken, NJ 07030, USA
John Wiley & Sons, The Atrium, Southern Gate, Chichester, West Sussex, P019
    8SQ, United Kingdom
John Wiley & Sons (Canada) Ltd., 5353 Dundas Street West, Suite 400, Toronto,
    Ontario, M9B 6HB, Canada
John Wiley & Sons Australia Ltd., 42 McDougall Street, Milton, Queensland 4064,
    Australia
Wiley-VCH, Boschstrasse 12, D-69469 Weinheim, Germany

Library of Congress Cataloging-in-Publication Data
ISBN 978–0–470–82508–2

Typeset in 11/14pt Goudy by Thomson Digital, India
Printed in Singapore by Saik Wah Press Pte. Ltd.
10 9 8 7 6 5 4 3 2 1

For Elainor, Anna, Alfie, and Chance

Contents

Preface

One of the nice things about working in an advertising agency is being invited to lots of cocktail parties. One of the other benefits is having access to a huge amount of consumer attitude and behavior data across a wide variety of business categories. In the course of a business day, I can attend meetings with a broad range of clients, and discuss even more diverse businesses back at the agency.

Making the mental leap from discussing beer drinkers straight into a graphic chat about feminine hygiene can be disconcerting. Then going on to meetings about shopping trends, laptop distribution issues, household detergent packaging, hair care range extensions, a new automobile launch, and some pro bono charity work, can make your head spin.

What sometimes happens, as with any creative process, is that big ideas gradually begin to form in your mind. James Webb Young, a wonderful copywriter in a bygone age, described ideas emerging in the mind like a tropical island slowly rising on the horizon of a vast ocean. Gradually getting closer and more distinct as the idea takes form and shape.

I live on a tropical island called Singapore, so perhaps it was natural that a big idea began to emerge in my mind when I was slightly inebriated at a pre-Christmas cocktail party. I was intrigued about the data I was seeing all pointing toward the same basic conclusion: fundamental attitudes and values seem to be changing, and consumers are starting to make buying decisions in a very different way.

Not all at the same time, and not all at the same speed, but certainly in the same direction.

The conspicuous consumption of the past century is being replaced by a much more considered buying process. I began to dig into the reasons for this change in behavior, and think about the implications. Many conclusions I had come to, which I assumed would take decades to occur, suddenly started to become reality in various places around the world, like small islands of change rising out of a sea of normality.

So I started thinking more broadly and projecting further into the future, digging and searching for clues about the lifestyle and business changes that will likely occur this century. I found that even my most far-fetched ideas and assumptions seemed to keep fitting with the values and behavior that will shape the twenty-first century. I kept finding snippets of evidence and validation for some of the major business and political changes that I believe will occur. Most worryingly it also became clear that we will face some significant moral and ethical dilemmas in the very near future.

However, crystal ball gazing is a dangerous profession. The balls have a habit of rolling off the table and shattering at the most inconvenient moment . . . usually when your brilliant vision of the future is contradicted by an inconvenient fact. So this book will stay well away from specific, outlandish predictions and focus on the major trends that will shape the twenty-first century, and their implications.

However, I can't help but see some really interesting potential developments such as Sony and Panasonic being the biggest automobile manufacturers within 15 years, and Vodafone and T-Mobile becoming the biggest publishers of newspapers and magazines.

Plus the likelihood that we'll soon be drinking our own urine in self-sufficient, carbon-neutral, extended-family homes.

But let's not get ahead of ourselves. Let's look at the trends and see where they lead us. Some big demographic and attitudinal changes will shape the twenty-first century, which will combine and overlap to create a very different type of behavior and lifestyle.

I want this book to be of interest to everyone who is curious about what the twenty-first century may bring, so I have tried to avoid using business language, and I do make some sweeping generalizations. My apologies in advance to academics and businessmen who may prefer more precision and data.

I hope you find this book thought provoking and able to provide some insights into the new Age of Selfish Altruism.

Acknowledgments

Many of the forecasts and ideas were stimulated by articles I found by accessing WPP Group sources, particularly those by Ann Mack, Director of Trendspotting at JWT and her intelligence group who were inspirational. The website is http://www.jwtintelligence.com.

In addition, the daily global media monitoring service delivered by TNS provided a constant source of interesting news which helped support the hypothesis of this book.

I would also like to thank C.J. Hwu at John Wiley & Sons (Asia) who convinced me that I should write a book and provided constant motivation to get me to actually complete it.

David Rule was a ruthless editor who straightened out a lot of my meandering anecdotes to make the book a far better read.

Koh Hwee Peng very kindly provided all the charts, graphs and illustrations.

Finally, thanks to my wife Elainor who suffered more than the usual pain of living with me during the gestation of this tome.

*Always read something that will make
you look good if you die in the middle of it.*

—P.J. O'Rourke

Introduction

SELFISHNESS: *the act of placing one's own needs or desires above the needs or desires of others.*

ALTRUISM: *the deliberate pursuit of the interests or welfare of others, or the public interest.*

The twenty-first century is being increasingly underpinned by a new morality and social consensus, which is changing the way we live. A new society is emerging that lives differently, thinks differently, and acts differently from the aggressive, egotistical consumerism of the twentieth century.

Several long-term mega-trends are combining with short-term events to create a new consumer who will radically change the global economy over the course of the next few decades. What they buy, why they buy, and how they buy will all undergo fundamental change. Old manufacturing methodology will need to be cast aside along with stereotyped marketing techniques and traditional sales structures. Companies will need to change the way they are organized radically from integrated, hierarchical, top-down conglomerates, to bottom-up, user-driven, coordinators of demand-driven manufacture. Most importantly, marketers will be forced to consider the new values and morals of the twenty-first-century consumer, or face significant market decline.

GDP assumptions and social service provisions will need to be reassessed as citizens' age increases and population declines in several of the world's most important countries. Continual GDP growth will no longer be feasible or realistic for many nations, and learning how to maintain welfare standards in the face of economic decline will become a critical challenge to government competence.

Twenty-first-century "post-consumers" will be more communal and ethical in their attitudes and aspirations. Conspicuous consumption will become a thing of the past, and "real values" will dominate purchase patterns and behavior. Consumers will want what is best for themselves, but not at the cost of others. It will herald an Age of Selfish Altruism.

It's a new global morality. It's happening now. And it's happening at a faster pace than expected.

1 The Lifecycle

This is the dawning of the Age of Aquarius.
"Aquarius" from the musical *Hair*

When I was a lot younger, I heard this song about the dawning of the Age of Aquarius, from the musical *Hair*. For years I wondered, what on earth was the Age of Aquarius? How would I know when I was in it? What difference would it make to my life?

The only clues were contained in the lyrics, which weren't particularly helpful:

> *When the moon is in the Seventh House and Jupiter aligns with Mars, then peace will guide the planets and love will steer the stars.*

I really aspired to live in the Age of Aquarius, and perhaps I do. Perhaps we are all now living in the Age of Aquarius, but we just don't realize it!

Various eras are described by the overwhelming change in values or technology that occurred in that period. These periods are often referred to as an "age": the Stone Age; the Dark Ages; the Age of Enlightenment; the Age of Reason; the Steam Age; the Digital Age.

These ages describe a fundamental new innovation, set of values, or lifestyle that created a change in mass behavior. We talk about being in the Digital Age at present because digitization is affecting so many aspects of our life: from communication to entertainment, and household appliances to work practices.

It's easy to describe an age when it is based on new technology. People in the nineteenth century knew that they were in the Steam Age, because that new source of energy made a significant difference to people's lives. Having immense power on tap allowed mass production of goods, and the means to transport them. The steam ship supplanted the sailing vessel, steam trains derailed the horse and cart, and steam powered the Industrial Revolution.

When an age is based on a new set of values or beliefs, it is a lot harder to recognize. This is why many ages are identified later. Often an age is named by historians who look back on the values or behavior of a period and characterize it in a certain way. Did people in the Age of Reason think they were living in the Age of Reason? Probably not. People who were living in the Age of Enlightenment, and contributed to its thinking and new ideals, probably didn't think they were living in the Age of Enlightenment. They may have embodied all of its values, but it was only later that historians coined the name.

I believe that we're entering a period that we should call the Age of Selfish Altruism. The dilemma we will all face is between doing what's best for ourselves and doing what's best for everyone else.

Last century, we lived in a dog-eat-dog, competitive world. Greed was good. We were solely motivated by our selfish needs and damn the consequences. This resulted in powerful economic growth and many people's standard of living improving dramatically. But it came at the cost of huge environmental damage, a shrinking and disintegrating family unit, and ebbing faith and conscience.

The twenty-first century is already showing that we are developing the personal values and political will to reverse this situation. Concern for the planet will affect almost every aspect of our lives this century, and it is a key value and behavioral indicator of the Age of Selfish Altruism. Concern for the environment will affect purchase patterns, lifestyles, politics, and business. I believe that we will, together, build a healthier, sustainable lifestyle, and a more rewarding way of life built on decency and self respect.

I wish we could call it the Age of Aquarius. But who knows, if we save the planet and develop a new way of living, later historians may yet give it that moniker!

The End of the Oil Age

As Sheikh Yamani, the former OPEC minister, once said to his colleagues, "The Stone Age didn't end because they ran out of stones." He was absolutely right. The Age of Steam didn't come to an end because we ran out of water and fuel. Oil simply offered a better alternative to steam, so we gradually moved from a nineteenth-century Steam Age to the oil-powered age of the twentieth century.

The Oil Age will soon reach its peak, and begin to decline as Sheik Yamani predicts, but not because of a single alternative mineral or new technology, but because of a matrix of "sustainable" energy sources and changing consumer purchase habits.

A major concern that has faced the world for the past few years has been whether there were sufficient oil reserves to meet ever-increasing global needs. Oil prices rose as demand outstripped supply, and concerns about reserves and production mounted. This will soon change as individuals and countries aggressively pursue more energy-efficient and sustainable options, so we may well have already *passed* the peak in global oil demand.

As the world changes to sustainable energy sources, electric cars, and the huge range of other energy-saving practices, it will eventually reduce demand for oil. The speed with which this occurs is difficult to estimate, but we know that major reductions in carbon emissions will occur over the next decade, and accelerate beyond that.

So if 2008 wasn't already the year that oil production peaked, it is not far away. Burning fossil fuels is creating a threat to the entire planet, so alternatives simply have to be found, or the world as we know it may simply not be viable in the near future. The search for ways to achieve alternative, sustainable energy is driving technological and attitudinal change around the world. We must not underestimate the effect that environmental concern is now playing in peoples' minds, technology development, corporate life, and government policy.

It is a central driver of change, and will require the complete transformation of many companies, categories and industries, or they will simply decline and disappear. This will bring to an end many of the ages that were so central to the twentieth century, and have played such a big part in our lives.

The Product Lifecycle

If we look at the growth and subsequent decline of any Age, era, or product, we can see that they have a lifecycle, rather like a bell curve in appearance.

Each new Age offers an array of new values or a new technology that gradually picks up adherents, and enjoys steady growth among "early adopters." Then it reaches a point at which it develops mass-market appeal, and there is a dramatic increase in adherents. This wave of acceptance rises up the leading edge of the bell curve and accelerates strongly, creating a massive group of supporters. Total acceptance is reached at the top of the bell curve, when a set of values or a new technology becomes the standard for an entire population. However, nothing can stay at the top of the curve forever, and decline begins for any of a thousand reasons. The decline can be slow and steady or precipitously steep, until the bottom edge of the curve is reached and the Age comes to an end, or the technology is no longer useful (see figure 1.1).

Everyone feels secure in their existing age and with technology that they are familiar with. It is human nature to see all the problems that a new technology will face, and the issues that new inventions need to address are certainly real. Even at the beginning of the twentieth century it must have felt as though the steam engine would be a permanent fixture to the end of time. Oil killed steam. Within just a

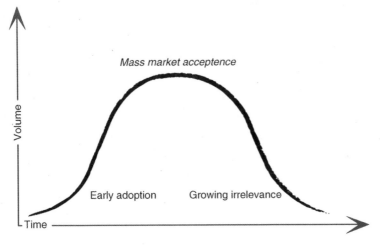

Figure 1.1 The product lifecycle

few decades, the oil-powered diesel engine had replaced steam propulsion in ships and locomotives.

I noted in the *Wall Street Journal* an editorial that said about electric cars: "It is unclear whether Americans will embrace electric vehicles and when the market will be ready for them." It went on to give the reasons for their skepticism, including the likelihood that electric cars would be smaller than the roomier models that US buyers favor, the need for recharging, the lack of an infrastructure of recharging stations, and new repair shops. I bet they said the same thing 100 years ago about combustion-engine automobiles!

When an invention is clearly able to offer a significant advantage over existing products, it is only a matter of time before the new technology begins to destroy the existing one. And a new Age begins.

Sometimes a product becomes technologically outmoded, like photographic film or boxy TVs. Sometimes a brand becomes out of touch with the changing values or behavior of its users and offers a less relevant appeal. Whatever the reason, I don't know of a single Age or product type that has set off on the downward slope of the bell curve and managed to recover. Once an Age, brand, or product type is on the way out, it doesn't come back up the bell curve again. And the only way for a *brand* to stay on the top of the bell curve of mass appeal is continuous innovation of new product forms, and transformational change when new values emerge.

Marketers refer to this bell curve effect as being a product lifecycle. Although there is general acceptance that all brands and even product categories have lifecycles, there is much debate about how they can be extended.

How Brands Beat the Bell Curve

Many marketing books and manuals provide advice about keeping brands forever "young." They claim that no brand needs to age, and can maintain their youthful vigor. Coca-Cola, Gillette, Tide detergent, Ivory soap, and even McDonald's are offered as examples of perpetually young brands.

What this really means is that if a brand wants to stay at the top of the curve, it needs to provide constant product innovation and continued relevance to its core user group.

McDonald's, for example, was about to face serious decline as its product offering had become very staid, and it was increasingly out of touch with new consumer values. The company long ignored obvious changing attitudes toward healthier eating and failed to make menu changes despite increasing criticism and even a movie that derided the brand. McDonald's seemed locked in its attitudes and traditional offerings, and simply soldiered on in the face of mounting criticism and softening sales. The convenience food category was also seeing beef burgers accounting for a declining share of the overall market with an increasing demand for "healthier" white meats such as chicken and fish.

In addition, total "out of home" consumption was being made more competitive by the dramatic growth of Starbucks, sushi bars, sandwich shops, and a host of new food and beverage outlets.

McDonald's finally saw the light. It modified its menu by offering salads and healthier foods, and broadened its distribution with the creation of new McCafes. The brand has not moved away from its core promise of fast, convenient, low-cost food, but stayed relevant to new customer needs through product innovation and broader distribution. By catering to these new needs of consumers, the company is now enjoying the increased sales and financial benefits that the change in its behavior has generated. McDonald's transformed its product offering and distribution, and has been able to stay on top of the growth curve and avoid the slippery downward slope which it was peering down just a few years ago.

Turning to the bar soap category, we can all see that solid bar soaps are being eroded by liquid soaps and shower gels. Bar soaps are in the mature, downward slope of their lifecycle bell curve. The Ivory brand, for example, is still powerful, but it has undergone a change in physical form, and is transitioning from the dying solid soap category to the still youthful liquid soap market.

Dove also began life as a bar of soap, but it has been transformed into a range of personal care products from cleansers to moisturizers to antiperspirants. The brand has been faithful to its brand promise of being kind to skin, but its delivery of this promise has expanded from bars to liquids, creams, and aerosols.

So a brand can stay young, but only if it has a clear vision of the values it offers to its customers, and only if it constantly innovates to keep pace with changing attitudes and product form lifecycles.

Even Coca-Cola is introducing a green tea-flavored product in Japan to appeal to more health-conscious young women. Nothing is sacred if it wants to survive!

Failing to Adapt

Companies that transform themselves and adapt to technological change and shifting consumer needs will stay at the top of the bell curve. Those that fail to transform their business model, and remain fixed to their original technology will slowly die as they age along with the category.

Kodak and other providers of silver-halide photographic film, which have failed to transform themselves adequately into providers of digital imagery, are rapidly dying along with the category they built. They are the steam-engine manufacturers of this century, locked in an old technology.

Even those photographic equipment manufacturers who have changed their product offering from film to digital are now under pressure from mobile phones and other handheld devices that offer built-in cameras. So merely changing from film to digital isn't enough of a transformation to guarantee the survival of camera companies. They need to look at the entire world of digital imagery, not just the narrow market of cameras, which are just one possible photographic tool.

Recognizing when an Age is about to end, or when a category is about to begin its decline is not really difficult. Many companies can clearly see their nemesis, but choose to ignore it, or rationalize why it is less threatening than it seems. They are able to do this because there is often a period of several years between the emergence of a new product and its broad-scale market adoption. During this period, a company's sales growth can often be sustained, and it comes to believe its illusions.

Technological change that brings a particular product, category, or age to an end emerges slowly as all the components to make it successful take time to develop.

The PC took a long time to reach its current ubiquity. It required the connectivity of the internet, the power of the silicon chip, the development of effective operating systems, and a host of other complementary technologies to help it rise up to the top of its bell curve. Most manufacturers of mainframe computers refused to acknowledge the PC as a threat to their business customer base during the time of its early development, and derided the prospect of home computing as a "fantasy."

The result was that those mainframe manufacturers that failed to transform their product offering and adapt their business model simply withered away. Their old mainframe technology and service contract business model had become irrelevant to business customers in a new microchip and PC world. I'm sure that many mainframe manufacturers eventually saw the PC threat to their existence, but simply failed to make the massive commitment to change that was necessary. Perhaps only IBM had the vision, courage, and commitment to transform itself totally into a very different, leading-edge company.

A Century of Change

Oil and electricity powered the twentieth century and allowed the creation of motor cars, airplanes, armaments, communications and a plethora of new consumer goods. Oil also enabled the creation of new chemical industries, which produced films, plastics, fertilizers, and an array of human-made fibers.

These were the building blocks for a consumer lifestyle that was unimaginable 100 years ago. It is important to review the impact that technology has had on the past century. This will allow us to understand the development of the consumer society that we currently live in, but are about to leave.

By looking at the technological changes that are occurring in key consumer goods categories, we can see exactly where these industries are on their bell curve or lifecycle, and anticipate some of the changes that will soon occur. Some companies and business categories are reinventing themselves or finding new products to cater to changing needs. Others seem to be bewildered by change and are failing to transform their products or business model. It takes courage and foresight to change the long-term direction of a company completely when investors and stakeholders demand optimum short-term performance and consistent profits. Meeting shareholder expectations while delivering long-term transformation is an extraordinarily difficult management skill, but without it, companies soon begin to slip down the aging far side of the bell curve.

Changes in product lifecycles are not only affected by new technology, but are also driven by different consumer behavior. When the value system of a consumer changes, or new ethical standards evolve, this can dramatically affect what people buy, why they buy, and how they buy. A product, even if it is on the leading edge, that fails to meet the ethical or moral standards of its users can quickly go from being completely relevant to a relic of a previous Age. So companies need to stay abreast of consumer values as well as create technical innovation. This task has become more urgent because values are changing and innovations occurring at a faster and faster pace. The monitoring of these changes has never been easier. The challenge is in knowing what to do!

This book will describe how a combination of category changes and new postconsumer values will shape the twenty-first century, and create very different lifestyles. These changes offer both challenge and opportunity for businesses and the products and services they sell. A surprising number of companies and categories are facing the prospect of either transforming their business and products, or suffering a rapid decline in their fortunes.

The combination of environmental concerns, post-consumer attitudes, aging global populations, and new standards of consensus building are creating a different "post-consumer" and a new Age of Selfish Altruism.

2

Twentieth-
Century Ages

The twentieth century could be described in many ways, because it saw more changes in lifestyle, technology, and behavior than have ever been seen before in history. The previous century spawned several technology "ages," which are now in different stages of their bell-curve development. Some will continue to affect the twenty-first century, but many brands, product forms, entire business categories will soon be confined to history.

It was only when I began writing this book that I fully realized the enormous changes that are already in progress, and those about to occur in the very near future. We often aren't aware of how groundbreaking or lifestyle-changing certain events are, because they creep up on us as natural, normal developments in our regular lifestyle. This is due to the bell-curve effect, where new developments gain increasing acceptance, and keep gaining adherents, until using the new product seems completely normal to all of us. Yet only a few years before, purchasing the new product seemed such a huge step forward into the unknown.

When we were still using film in our cameras, the change to a digital camera seemed liked a very big step indeed. But once we began using a digital camera we simply couldn't imagine how we ever used to fiddle around loading rolls of celluloid into the back of an unwieldy camera, and then have to take it out and get it "developed." Today, it's hard even to find film or film cameras, and the entire category has been forgotten. It seems such a natural, normal transition that we don't appreciate the traumatic change that this created in the industry that manufactured film and cameras, the retailers who sold the products, and the companies that developed the film and produced prints. Yet this change was fully anticipated, and companies that were going to be affected had plenty of time to change their business model if they wanted to stay in business. Unfortunately, many didn't.

Let's take a look at the most important and influential Ages of the twentieth century and the stage of bell-curve development that they are currently in.

The Age of the Automobile

Any color—so long as it's black.
—Henry Ford

The invention of the internal-combustion engine created a giant industry devoted to providing personal transportation for the world's population. For much of the past century, the largest corporations were directly related to the manufacture and movement of automobiles powered by internal combustion engines: General Motors (GM), Ford, Toyota, Nissan, Renault, Fiat, VW, Daimler, BMW; Exxon, Shell, BP, Total, Chevron; Goodyear, Pirelli, Bridgestone; Bosch, Lucas, Denso, and literally thousands of other companies with millions of employees.

Automobile manufacturers are so integral to the economic health of many countries that in 1955, Charlie Wilson, the CEO of GM would say that "what was good for our country was good for General Motors and vice versa. The difference did not exist. Our company is too big. It goes with the welfare of the country."

This is often misquoted as "What is good for General Motors, is good for America." Although there is less bravado in the actual statement to Congress by Wilson, the underlying meaning is the same: the economic health of the US could be directly related to the prosperity of GM. And vice versa.

Think for a moment about how much of the world's economic wealth is directly related to the automobile. How many jobs and incomes are tied to its manufacture, sales and propulsion? How many communities, cities, and countries' economies are reliant on the automobile?

Whatever the answer, one thing is for sure, the age of the internal-combustion engine is coming to an end! The petrol-driven car has reached the top of its bell curve and is now about to head down the far side. It won't be a massive and precipitous slide, in which all petrol cars disappear like dinosaurs in an asteroid strike. There will be markets where growth continues, particularly those with big geographies and in the less economically developed markets. And there will be good years and bad as gasoline prices and economic cycles affect demand. However, the whole personal transportation industry is being affected by two fundamentals: environmental concerns and technological breakthrough.

Environmental issues are no longer something that countries can simply talk about, they have become extremely urgent and immediate action is now demanded of both government and manufacturers. Ecological concerns are driving increasingly aggressive legislation and forcing great change on the auto industry.

The state of California has often been a leader in the legislation for cleaner air and less pollution from automobiles after smog blanketed LA for many years. Where California leads, the nation usually follows. Unleaded fuel, catalytic converters and higher gas mileage were all demanded by California and then adopted across the US.

Governor Arnold Schwarzenegger has traded in his gas-guzzling, top of the line Humvee, which was so much part of his persona, and become a powerful environmental advocate. He has mandated that automobiles sold in his state must have an average of 35.5 miles per gallon (mpg) by 2016, and President Barack Obama has now adopted that as a national objective. Although this is a laudable effort, China already has a mandate of 43mpg for its cars, and the EU has a target of 47mpg by 2012. The pressure on automobile manufacturers will continue to be more and more intense as they are such an obvious and significant source of carbon dioxide pollution.

As a result of this environmental pressure, technological break-throughs are finally making battery-powered vehicles a realistic alternative to the internal-combustion engine. Lithium-ion batteries, which are lighter and more durable, have dramatically improved the viability of electric cars. This technology breakthrough will start to change the nature of the automobile industry, much as the silicon chip enabled the development of PCs. The silicon chip went through a decade of development until it was many times more powerful than the early models, and battery technology will do the same.

Going Electric

Electric cars will largely replace petrol-driven vehicles in the same way as PCs overwhelmed mainframe computers. It may take a decade, or more, but it will happen. Gasoline prices will affect the growth of "greener" vehicles. The lower prices at time of writing this book, have already adversely affected the sales of the more fuel-efficient and greener Toyota Prius in the US.

It is therefore logical that every time gas prices rise, electric cars will thrive, but in times of lower gas prices they will have to compete with traditional vehicles more on the basis of price and design. So electric cars will initially make their presence felt most acutely in affluent markets where petrol prices are consistently high and geographies small.

Cities will be affected earlier than rural communities, because range and easy rechargeability will be an issue in first-generation electric cars. Many cities, such as London, have a congestion charge for vehicles entering their urban center, but this fee is waived for clean, electric vehicles. Electric cars, even with a limited range, will be far cheaper to operate than those with petrol power, and they can be easily recharged at home every evening.

Countries with high gasoline prices will be early adopters. Most European countries have significant taxes on gasoline, so even when global oil prices are low, the pump prices remain high. Europeans will find that electric cars will reduce their running costs significantly, as well as help reduce the carbon footprint of both the individual and the country.

First-world countries that can afford the higher entry price of electric cars should also be early buyers, rather than third-world markets. Governments that have signed up to various treaties and protocols to reduce greenhouse gases will likely provide significant tax incentives and subsidies to encourage electric car development and purchase. This will result in a closer price relationship between electric- and gasoline-powered vehicles. We can therefore expect major US urban centers, and many European countries, especially Benelux, plus Asian city states such as Singapore and Hong Kong to be the most aggressive early adopters.

A key indicator of the potential for greener vehicles is in Japan, where the Toyota Prius became the top-selling individual brand in early 2009. And in mid-2009, when global automobile sales were recording massive declines and manufacturers facing bankruptcy, Toyota's Prius factory was in overtime producing a record 1.1 million new vehicles for 2010 global sales.

Global research by Synovate asked car buyers if money were no object would they prefer to buy a green car, or a dream car, or a regular petrol powered vehicle? The clear preference across all 18 markets surveyed was to buy a green car, with 37 percent of respondents saying this would be their preferred purchase. Thirty-one percent said they would buy their dream car, but of this total 22 percent claimed that "my dream car *is* a green car." This meant that 59 percent—or very nearly six in ten people—showed the clear desire to go green.

Further evidence of the interest in electric cars and the aspiration for green technology was found in a recent survey by the Royal Automobile Club in the UK. The results of the survey indicated that 20 percent of current car owners were either planning to buy an electric car, or would consider doing so.

It is quite clear that there is a strong consumer desire for "greener" cars, whether hybrid or electric, and this is being encouraged by government action in many countries. The UK government, for example, will begin offering grants of up to £5,000 to help sales of electric cars, but doesn't expect to see a mass market until 2017 or later. Electric cars may be slow to gain a significant share of the total automobile market, but this is always the case with new technologies as they set off on the early stages of their development. But make no mistake about it, once battery cars begin the rapid climb up the bell curve of mass acceptance, the trend will be inexorably down for the petrol-driven car, and all that will matter for the auto industry is the rate of decline.

IBM Global Business Services forecast electric cars will account for less than 5 percent of the global market by 2015. That may sound small, but it's a heck of a lot of cars! And if you're an electric car manufacturer that only needs to sell 10,000 or 20,000 units to make a good profit, you'll be in a serious expansion mode. The growth of the personal computer market was slow at first as it crept along the leading edge of its bell curve, but then as costs declined, chips became more powerful, and functionality improved, it started to accelerate up that steep gradient of mass acceptance.

Similarly, the growth of online retailing has been described as disappointingly low, having reached only a 5 percent share of all retail transactions in the US in 2008, according to Forrester Research. But this is still a sales volume of more than $140 billion! This far exceeds the volume forecasts of e-tailers and researchers earlier in the decade. Online shopping is still in its early bell-curve stage, and increasing bandwidth will enable a host of new tools to add excitement to the online shopping experience.

For example, virtual tours of shops will provide the ability to see products in 3D and examine them from different angles. Or it will be possible to achieve the virtual placement of furniture or other items in your home, so you can see how they look "in situ" before buying. There is already the ability to change the color of an item instantly, or to "see yourself in clothing" that you can share with your friends before actually purchasing. New technology like this always drives strong growth, and the electric car market will be no different.

A Slow Start but a Promising Future

It is inevitable that the electric car market will get off to a slow start despite massive publicity and hullabaloo. The "failure to live up to expectations" happens with all new technologies. It is invariably followed by the media commenting that acceptance of electric cars has been far lower than expected and the petrol engine is still king.

But as second- and third-generation vehicles powered by improved battery technology hit the market, the electric car will overwhelm petrol engines in the same way that cars outpaced horse drawn buggies a century ago. Some automobile manufacturers really see the future. Carlos Ghosn, the CEO of Renault-Nissan recently said that any car using oil was "unsustainable."

"I want a pure electric car," said Ghosn. "It's going to be zero emissions." He has already agreed that Nissan's major factory in the UK will be converted to electric car manufacture.

BMW is spending $1 billion to create a small car that will include an electric version. "We in the auto industry have the internal combustion engine so strongly fixed in our minds that we think it will last forever. I don't believe that," said BMW CEO Norbert Reithofer.

New Toyota president Akio Toyoda says, "We are in a once-in-a-century transformation of the automobile market. And what is clear to me is that what is going to happen will not just be an extension of the past."

The advent of electric cars with their renewable energy sources will devastate brands and industries reliant on gasoline-powered engines and oil-powered facilities. How many of these companies will quickly transform their business, and how many will simply wither and die like the horse-drawn carriage makers a hundred years ago? Or steam-engine manufacturers? What happens to manufacturers of internal-combustion engines, spark plugs, and all the components an old-technology engine contains? None are necessary in an electric car. All these industries will need to transform or face inexorable erosion of their business.

Many automobile companies are still far too obsessed with short-term changes in market conditions, design preferences, and emerging market opportunities. They seem to assume that the playing field will not change radically. But more than 50 new brands of electric car are scheduled to hit the US market before 2012! Some of these will come from Ford, BMW, Nissan, and Toyota, but the entry of a whole new array of brands will provide a range of choice that consumers have not enjoyed for decades.

Again, we can draw parallels with the PC industry, which spawned hundreds of startup businesses. But as the market grew, the winners soon emerged while others found the pace too hot. Much has to do with distribution and marketing, but critical criteria will include cost, design, and functionality. However, the most important competitive characteristic from the very outset will be governed by battery technology and electronic capability. The battery, and its ability to store power, will be absolutely critical to many of the most important developments of the twenty-first century.

Small, powerful batteries that can provide sufficient power for extended use have already transformed many product categories, notably mobile phones and laptops. Any portable object requiring extended use away from a fixed power source needs a battery. The new breed of lithium-ion batteries delivered the power required by portable equipment, and now that same technology will power automobiles.

Batteries the Key

We often see industry technology crossover, such as computer manufacturers entering the mobile phone market. Soon we will see consumer electronic giants provide the key technology for automobiles. Consumer electronics companies may actually become automobile manufacturers.

Panasonic bought Sanyo for $9 billion in late 2008. Sanyo is the world's leading lithium-ion battery manufacturer. Panasonic now provides Toyota with batteries for its hybrid vehicles, including the Prius. Nissan has hooked up with NEC in a $1 billion battery joint venture. Mitsubishi and Yuasu Corporation are jointly building a ¥10 billion factory to mass produce large-size lithium-ion batteries to supply Mitsubishi Motors i-Miev electric cars. LG is providing the battery technology to Korean electric car manufacturers, and is already planning a Detroit location for its factory in America.

The US government is keenly aware that leadership in battery technology is critical not only to cars, but a whole range of environmentally sensitive industries. So expect massive public/private partnerships devoted to battery technology and manufacture to emerge in the US, as well as many other countries. The US has allocated $2.4 billion in grants for advanced battery manufacturing and $25 billion in low-interest loans to encourage the development of environmentally friendly vehicles. The US government has already received 165 applications for battery-related grants. The governor of Michigan is offering another $355 million of tax credits to help make her state become "the battery capital of the world."

The question we have to ask is should governments be supporting traditional car manufacturers as the entire industry paradigm is about to change? Are governments pouring money into huge companies that may become minor players in just a few short years? The chances of the taxpayer funds that are currently being plowed into automobile companies being repaid seems highly unlikely given the major transition to electric cars that will happen within a decade. Ten years for GM to repay $50 billion seems an unlikely prospect, no matter how much restructuring has been done.

The advent of electric cars will create a new playing field on which everyone is starting at pretty much the same level. Existing manufacturers theoretically have some advantage with their manufacturing capability, supplier chain, dealer network, and automotive market knowledge. However, these advantages could become a liability if the business model of current manufacturers doesn't change to meet new consumer needs. If current automotive brands try to maintain their present mode of manufacture and distribution, merely substituting electric for petrol engines, I fear that they will lose out heavily as the market goes electric.

An electric car is an opportunity to develop new manufacturing techniques, new materials, and new distribution methods. All the newly formed electric car brands have a very small team of employees, most of whom are project managers and designers. Manufacturing is outsourced. All components are purchased from partner companies that can provide manufacturing capability. New developments are undertaken on a project basis by consultants or component suppliers. The operating philosophy of these new electric car companies is to minimize fixed costs and capital outlays. Stay consumer-focused and assignment-driven. Use temporary staff on a project basis, rather than full-time departmental employees. For example, a California electric car company called Coda Automotive has only 15 engineering employees. The car itself is assembled in China using a Mitsubishi chassis, Delphi power steering, BorgWarner transaxle, a charging device from Lear, and lights, hood, and bumpers from Porsche design. Oh yes, and a battery from Tianjin Lishen.

These new automobile companies will have no "automotive plants" or massive unionized employee structures. They will be nimble, consumer-focused, low-cost producers, which may choose to sell direct instead of through dealers. They will be the automotive equivalent of Dell computers. Electric car manufacturers will be able to design and manufacture a new car in less than half the time it takes existing automotive companies to produce a new petrol-powered vehicle. And eventually, they will build to order, as does Dell. Think of the build-to-order opportunities for electric car brands if they dispense with "fixed assembly line" thinking and operations!

New battery car brands can use online purchasing and open-source manufacture to become truly consumer-centric, with considerable manufacturing flexibility and low overheads. This could give new, battery-powered car manufacturers cost-competitiveness over traditional, hierarchical companies, which have legacy manufacturing plants, long-term supplier partnerships, and fixed dealer networks.

So we should picture GM as being in the same position as IBM when it was still a mainframe manufacturer. GM is clearly facing a transformational change in the automobile market with hybrid and electric powered cars replacing the internal combustion engine. In the same way, IBM was faced with low-cost, ever more powerful PCs, which would soon become the choice of its business customers, instead of high-cost mainframes, with all the associated servicing costs and application inflexibility. IBM totally transformed its business. Burroughs, ICL, Univac, and most other mainframe manufacturers failed to do so, and therefore dwindled or died.

Can GM or Ford totally transform itself into a nimble, consumer-centric builder of electric cars? My feeling is that their only hope is to set up an entirely separate business, "Ford Electric" for example. The management of this business would have full access to Ford's manufacturing capability, supplier relationships, and dealer network, but it would *not* be forced to use any of them. Ford Electric would benchmark itself against other electric cars, not simply be an addition to the total Ford model line-up. Ford Electric must be prepared to create an entirely new business model if that is what the market demands. They must look for the optimum business strategy, not just put a different engine in the same old car, which is manufactured in the same old way.

Electric cars will likely be sold in a different manner to petrol cars. The point-of-sales focus will likely be on recharging time, reliability, and emissions, not horsepower, mileage and a new grille. It will be a sales focus that is more rational than emotional. The method of manufacture will almost certainly be different with small volume, personalized production. And the sales and distribution process may be different, with a strong online emphasis and factory-to-door delivery.

So if Ford really wants to transform itself for the future, it needs to create this separate company and give it the mandate to build a whole new business to replace that of the old combustion-engine autos. I had Ford as a client for many years, so I truly hope that it has the same commitment to radical change that occurred at IBM, and does not try to "manage the transition" as Kodak did. Electric cars will open up a whole new world in the personal transportation sector, and existing auto manufacturers will need to transform their business model totally or gradually wither away.

Changes in the Market

Although China is now the world's largest market for cars, the government is strongly supporting the domestic manufacturers of electric cars. Warren Buffett has invested in a Chinese company called BYD, a battery manufacturer that is now producing electric cars. He and his partners believe that BYD could become the largest automaker in the world, based on its battery technology. In addition, they believe it could also be a leader in solar energy because BYD uses battery technology to store power from solar panels. Interestingly, BYD's batteries currently power iPods, iPhones, and computers. Equally importantly, BYD is pouring resources into developing a completely recyclable battery. VW is so impressed that it is now seeking partnership opportunities with BYD, again showing the new alliances that will be necessary to successfully compete in the electric car market.

Daimler has purchased 10 percent of Tesla, a Silicon Valley-based electric car startup. Mitsubishi is reported to be providing its i-MiEV electric cars to Peugeot Citroen. Mitsubishi will have five models in the market by 2013, and expects to have its electric car business in the black that same year with the sale of just 30,000 models. It's all change as we enter a new era. The fun is only just beginning as we leave the Age of the Motorcar, and enter a new world of personal transportation vehicles!

The psychology of electric car buyers is also likely to be very different from that of gas guzzler purchasers, especially in the early adopter stage of development. They will be more concerned with function than form, more focused on environmental benefits than on sexy design. How the car looks will be less important than how it is powered. There may even be a need for deliberately ugly hybrid and electric cars, so that their owners can be clearly seen to "prove" their commitment to reducing carbon emissions.

Car dealer networks will need to adapt quickly to this new world. Their sales techniques will need to adapt to cater to a more "serious" and concerned buyer, and their entire business model will have to change. Electric cars will require little or no regular servicing. So the dealer business model, which relies heavily on repeat servicing of petrol engines and supply of new parts, will have to find new revenue sources. Car sales will become one-off purchases, rather than extended relationships with ongoing revenue opportunities.

Perhaps the biggest danger facing car dealers is that consumers will likely start to buy online, which would allow them to "design their own car," and dealers will be mere delivery conduits. Or car dealerships may simply disappear altogether, along with the petrol-engined car, as relics of the past century.

UPS or Fedex can deliver cars that have been bought online, and there is no need to service the vehicle, so what is the use of a car dealer? Instead of physically going to see vehicles at a dealership, and having to imagine what your car will look like in the color you want, with the features you specify, consumers will be able to design and view their personal vehicle online. A buyer will simply log on to see the core design of the virtual car, and then select colors, trim, interiors, features, and components, and see the results immediately.

If marketers are smart, they will build online programs to let you virtually "drive" the car you've designed yourself through different scenarios: how does it look in town? How about in the countryside? How about at the beach? How will I look inside the car? What outfits will it go best with? This is the way cars should be sold, in the same way as, but much better than, buying a laptop computer online. Click to order and pay on your credit card, or download a loan application and submit online. Think of the cost savings without a dealer network and their added profit margin.

"No way," I hear many people cry. A buyer will always want to sit in the car, go for a test drive, and check how it feels. That is true, but I suspect that we will see "mega-dealerships" or "auto supermarkets" emerge that carry samples of 40 or 50 different brands of electric car, instead of individual brand dealerships. They will be pure retailers, selling the car and then saying goodbye until you return to buy again. How is a Ford dealer going to survive selling only one brand when an auto supermarket is offering 100 different ones? And once the sale is made, the dealer may never see the customer again, so there will be no recurring income. Maybe GM closing so many of its dealerships in the US did the owners a favor. Time to get into a different business, people!

The future of automobile sales will be with eBay and a huge range of online, interactive sales sites. Electric cars will also create new opportunities for all kinds of non-auto retailers, because electric cars need to be recharged frequently A regular home battery-charging process for an electric car will take up to four hours, but a fast "supercharge" can take less than 30 minutes. Retailers could offer free car "super charging" for customers. McDonald's is apparently already considering the opportunity to provide electric car-charging facilities for their customers. The ad man in me can already see the offer: "Free fill-up for your car with every McHappy meal." McDonald's could do for the electric car what Intel did for the laptop and power its development.

Shopping malls will offer a similar battery-charging service, or individual stores. "Free parking and free charging if you spend more than $20." The problem of how, where, and when to charge an electric car can be overcome easily if retailers seize the opportunity. The biggest issue will be what happens to the gas stations? Maybe Exxon will enter the burger market.

Finally, and most importantly, electric cars will have enormous consumer appeal for their unique driving characteristics versus petrol-engine cars. The consumer will not have to sacrifice any driving pleasure or learn new driving techniques. I drove the Mitsubishi i-MiEV, which is the first mass-produced electric vehicle, and it really has a "next generation" feel. When the power is turned on, there is no sound at all, just a "bing" to tell you that the battery has been activated as the dashboard lights up. The car drives like a subway train feels when it is leaving the station, with that surge of continuous electric power—without the noise. For those of you who are "car nuts": it has surprising and quite unexpected torque. The loudest sound is the noise of the tires on the road. No roar of an engine, or changing of gears. The weight distribution is also better because the battery provides a solid, stable feel to the car. All who test drove the car were blown away by the experience.

There will still be petrolheads who want to hear and feel the power of a V8 engine, but for most individuals and families who want a quiet and easy drive without any hassles or problems, they will opt for electric.

The biggest danger that the car represents is to pedestrians. Even on the test drive that I took, pedestrians were startled as we passed them because they didn't hear the noise of the car approaching. This is clearly going to be a problem for both pedestrians and the driver. The driver assumes that people hear their car approaching, which has always been the case with motor cars. When this doesn't happen, the driver has to be much more prepared for unexpected behavior by pedestrians and other vehicles. In Japan, electric car manufacturers have been asked to think about some sort of noise that can be emitted by the cars as a safety warning to pedestrians. Please Lord, let it not have anything to do with "Hello Kitty" or some other wacky Japanese manga character!

The Age of Flight

Ours is the commencement of a flying age, and I am happy to have popped into existence at a period so interesting.
—Amelia Earhart

The twentieth century was also the coming of Age of Flight. Aircraft went from propeller-driven, canvas and string single-seaters to giant metal and polymer people carriers; and from chugging biplanes to streamlined supersonic arrows. The new technology of the internal-combustion engine provided a power source that made commercial flying possible. The airline and automobile industries grew up together, and have increasingly refined their products to reach the top of their bell curves with the existing technology.

Air travel is now as commonplace as automobile transportation. Airline transportation costs have plummeted, with seating and service options for every kind of passenger. Airports have become more like luxurious shopping malls than transportation hubs, catering to a captive audience with time to kill. Flying has almost become something you spend your time doing between shopping malls. Airports are increasingly like mini-cities, with their own power generation, accommodation, transportation, security force, gardeners, electricians, plumbers, entertainment venues, shops, and restaurants.

The airline industry may not undergo the same kind of fundamental change that faces automobile manufacturers, but aircraft manufacturers will require foresight and flexibility to adapt to changing travel habits, new technology, and design innovation.

Lifting Bodies: the New Way to Fly

Boeing and Airbus dominate aircraft manufacture, but smaller companies are growing and springing up everywhere from China to Brazil, and Canada to Japan. They are catering to niche markets, such as executive jets, smaller-passenger-load aircraft, or "hybrid" planes, which can be converted easily to adapt to different passenger or cargo demands. However, they all use the same basic tube and wing design and engine technology. This current design of airplanes, and the engines that propel them, are now at the top of their bell curve, and are about to undergo change. Just as the electric car will revolutionize the automotive industry, so aircraft design and the nature of its engines will change over the next two decades. The basic design of subsonic passenger aircraft will begin to move away from the "tube and wing" appearance that we know so well, to a "lifting body," which will look very different.

The new generation of lifting-body aircraft will likely be based on the ideas and designs of Vincent Burnelli. Burnelli, who died in 1964, designed aircraft with a lifting body, which could carry a far greater payload than other aircraft types. He believed that all of the components of an aircraft should be used to maintain flight. Therefore, his fuselage section provided more than half the lift for the aircraft while cruising, as well as offering safer accommodation for passengers and crew. The fuselage was designed for maximum resistance to "telescoping," and being 60 percent of the weight and strength of the aircraft structure, provided far greater protection in the event of an accident.

His design has also been called a "flying wing," but his aircraft designs deliberately separated the passenger section from the fuel, engines, and other key components for maximum safety. Burnelli has many vocal supporters, who maintain that his lifting design has far greater safety, economic, and operational advantages over conventional "tube and wing" aircraft designs. His design philosophy was supported by many prominent civil and military aviation experts during his lifetime, but never gained political or economic acceptance. The most obvious reason is that Burnelli's designs seemed very unconventional, and didn't have the simplicity or ease of manufacture of the "tube and wing" style. But to this day, many conspiracy theorists believe that an aviation industry and government with vested interests in conventional "tube and wing" designs prevented the broadscale commercial acceptance of his aircraft.

However, Burnelli and his lifting-body idea may yet be vindicated, as some modern military aircraft, and even spacecraft, are incorporating his design concepts. For example the lifting-body characteristic that keeps the US space shuttle flying after re-entry is a direct application of Burnelli's design.

"Currently we use the tube and wing paradigm," said Dr. Juan J. Alonso, head of NASA's Fundamental Aeronautics program. "We've optimized the heck out of that concept. The Airbus A380 is almost as good as it can get." He believes that the "blended-wing body" looks like one of the best contenders for the future.

"Research is being conducted by NASA, Massachusetts Institute of Technology and Boeing, into a radically changed airframe which is similar in shape to a manta ray. The blended wing aircraft spreads out the fuselage, generating lift compared with the current airplane paradigm [tube and wing] in which lift is entirely generated by the wings. This immediately boosts fuel-efficiency and reduces noise," reported CNN recently.

Burnelli must be turning in his grave! Either from the excitement that his ideas are finally being adopted as commercially viable, or because the researchers haven't had the good grace to give him credit for his vision. So it is probable that the visual appearance of aircraft will change markedly when aircraft manufacturers finally decide to follow the ideas of Burnelli. Better lift means greater payload and higher profitability, so it is just a matter of time before a new generation of commercial aircraft emerges.

Interplanetary Travel?

Jules Verne also had a vision of another change likely to affect the airline industry in the first half of this century: the "spaceliner"—an aircraft that can fly through the stratosphere and into Earth orbit. It could do New York to Sydney in half an hour! Experimental suborbital aircraft will begin to offer tourist trips in the next couple of years, and as the technology evolves, there will be a progression to space flight, during which the craft can move into the Earth's low orbit. However, both engine technology and aircraft design are major issues that have to be overcome, and at a cost to make them commercially viable.

Sir Richard Branson has created The Spaceship Company, which will manufacture spacecraft for spaceliner operators. Its first customer is Virgin Galactic, which has been set up by Branson to provide space tourist flights. Another high-profile dreamer of spaceflight is Jeff Bezos, the founder of Amazon, who has invested in a company called Blue Origin. It was initially focused on suborbital spaceflight, with its New Shepard spacecraft design, which it planned to have in weekly commercial suborbital tourist service by 2010. Bezos claimed that Blue Origin is developing a suborbital space vehicle that will carry three or more astronauts to the edge of space. His company hopes to progress to orbital spaceflight and "step-by-step, to lower the cost of spaceflight so that many people can afford to go and we humans can better continue exploring the solar system." So interplanetary travel will finally emerge, many years after most people expected. The film *2001: A Space Odyssey* may be redated to 2012, or more likely 2021.

Although it is always fun to speculate and dream about changes to the design of aircraft, perhaps the biggest immediate change to affect the industry will come in the area of engine technology. Engines will change their fuel from kerosene to natural gas or electric engines, which will reduce carbon emissions to virtually zero. This will occur at the beginning of the next decade, and develop on a steady, progressive basis, until the entire industry has moved away from carbon-generating engines.

Qatar Airways is likely to be the first to have aircraft powered by natural gas, which is cleaner and probably cheaper than oil. The airline is working with Qatar Gas and Shell to produce a new generation engine, which will be carbon emission free. If successful, this would herald a shift toward natural gas, which would make airlines far greener and more environmentally safe.

Although further off than gas power, electric airline engines are also very viable for aircraft, and their development will happen in synchronization with the continuous technological advances of batteries and automobile engines. Either of these new engines will make the aircraft industry one of the least pollution-generating categories, which will be a relief to the industry because it has been the focus of increasing criticisms by environmentalists. The industry has also been under attack by governments, which have rationalized new airport taxes as "green taxes" to help offset the pollution caused by airlines and their passengers.

Will governments rescind these taxes for all aircraft with gas or electric engines, and reduce the cost of air travel? In your dreams. . . .

The Photographic Age

You push the button, we do the rest.
—George Eastman

The twentieth century saw the rise and fall of photographic film. George Eastman was the "Father of Photography," who perfected the roll film, which allowed the commercialization of silver-halide film. He then created a "pocket camera," allowing everyone the ability to record images of their families, friends, events, landscapes, flora, and fauna. His firm Kodak dominated the hardware and software of photography for most of the twentieth century.

Silver-halide film is now pretty much at the end of its life and is trailing along the final tail of its bell curve, killed by new digital technology. It is not as though everyone didn't see it coming. I was at a meeting in Hong Kong in 1993 where George Fisher the new CEO of Kodak predicted that one day cameras would be built into mobile phones and we would be able to send photos to each other. George was the ex-CEO of Motorola, so he could see the convergence of phone and camera technologies that was likely to occur.

The problem is that Kodak, as do all companies caught in old technologies, tried to eke out the profitable remains of their old film business while tiptoeing into the brave new digital world. Being half pregnant is a recipe for disaster! New technologies create different market conditions, and demand dramatic transformation to tear a company away from its existing business model. Products and services need to change; manufacturing and distribution need to adapt to different market conditions; sales and marketing need to develop a new customer base.

Sadly, few companies have the courage or ability to make such a dramatic change. They try to maintain their existing product range while developing new lines of business to meet the new market opportunities. This is simply not transformational enough. A company faced with category demise needs to change its entire business ethos completely to gear itself to the new world, and relegate or delegate its old business model to a "runout" team.

Kodak in my experience, "talked the talk," but it didn't "walk the walk." It talked and dedicated itself to the new digital world, but devoted most of its efforts to maximizing the returns on its old technologies. It assumed that its photographic heritage would give it a reputational advantage in the new digital-imaging arena. It believed that its photographic dealer-led business model would still be relevant in the new digital world.

The results speak for themselves:

- In 2001, Interbrand ranked Kodak the twenty-seventh-most valuable brand in the world, but by 2008 it wasn't even in the top 100.
- Kodak's share price declined from $34 in 2000 to $4 in 2008.
- Its revenue progressively declined from $14 billion in 2004 to $9 billion in 2008.
- It has reduced its workforce by more than 80 percent over the past few years.
- It has declared operating losses for the past six years through 2008 and into 2009.
- Kodak's annual advertising spend in the US was $202 million as recently as 2000. In 2008, it was measured at $30 million.
- After 116 years, Kodak stopped manufacturing film cameras in 2004.
- The company ceased production of its iconic Kodachrome film in 2009.

"It's still a highly recognized brand," said Jez Frampton, chief executive of Interbrand, "but you can't support a great brand without great products."

With the gradual disappearance of photographic film, an uncertain future for digital cameras, and intense competition in the printer market, what products will Kodak sell in the future? Kodak as a brand is gradually slipping off the consumer radar, and reaching the end of its product lifecycle.

I had Kodak as a client throughout the 1980s and 1990s. It was a company that had invariably charming, pleasant people to deal with, but it had an almost civil service culture that came from "owning" a category for much of the century. This created a layer of middle managers, and a slow-moving, bureaucratic structure. It clung to a deep commitment to chemicals, physical film, and paper prints despite clearly seeing that new digital technology would dramatically change the process of capturing and sharing images. It felt safety in "photography and film," and never seemed entirely comfortable with "digital imagery." It was a "brave new world" that it wanted to embrace, yet could never really make the emotional shift. There was also a certain arrogance in its belief that consumers would continue to see Kodak as the quality standard in imaging, and therefore assumed that its cameras and processes would be leaders in a new digital environment.

The entire industry completely changed. Not only has photographic film all but disappeared, but also cameras are increasingly being built into multifunction, handheld devices. There really isn't a photographic industry any more. Kodak is now reduced to advertising ink cartridges for digital printers! Once Kodak saw the digital train coming, it should have jumped aboard by redefining its entire business, probably through a merger or acquisition while it still had the cash and stock price to do so. Maybe George Fisher should have merged Kodak with his previous company, Motorola! Probably only a merger would have enabled Kodak to change its culture completely and transform the company.

Of course, hindsight is a wonderful thing. Kodak isn't alone in failing to make the transition to a digital world. There is a host of now defunct companies that manufactured reel-to-reel tape recorders, eight-track players, tape-cassettes, and VHS and Betamax videos, which all came and went. Whatever happened to Grundig? Using DVDs instead of prerecorded VHS tapes seemed like the most normal transition in the world. Remember how quickly typewriters disappeared as an entire product category with the advent of wordprocessors and then PCs? These new devices made typewriters redundant relics. Anyone remember Remington typewriters? Or even IBM typewriters? The transition from typewriter to wordprocessor and PC was so seamless we hardly noticed, because the benefits were so great.

This has also been the case as we transitioned easily and quickly from photographic film and prints, to digital cameras and images. Digital still cameras can now take videos. Handphones have still and video camera capability. Even the word "photograph" has a quaintly old-fashioned feel about it, and is used less and less in a world of digital "imagery." Camera manufacturers are also having difficulty in the Digital Age. Although they successfully transitioned from using film to employing memory cards, the camera itself is becoming increasingly specialized. Mobile phones are able to offer similar picture quality to cameras for "happy snaps," which form the majority of camera use. However, mobile phones have many additional functions unavailable on cameras such as being able to immediately send images to other people, and transmit photos to your laptop for storage. Cameras can't do all of that—yet.

There will likely always be a market for high-quality cameras, and cameras for specialist needs and functions. New developments like 3D images will extend the life of stand-alone cameras. However, increasingly, the mass market will move to mobile phones and handheld communication devices for their imaging needs. Nikon laid off 1,000 workers in early 2009 because of declining demand, and this trend will continue for all camera companies that fail to make the transition away from cameras as the core of their business. The demise of the photographic industry and the fate of those companies that failed to transform themselves in a new Digital Age must sound a warning to car manufacturers and a host of other twentieth-century industries.

The Golden Age of Entertainment

You ain't seen nothing yet.
—Al Jolson

The advent of the radio brought live entertainment into homes for the first time. The impact that radio had in the first half of the twentieth century was only matched by the arrival of television in the second half. Electricity in every home enabled the spread of radio, television, and a whole subsequent range of entertainment products. A show that might have been enjoyed by a live audience of hundreds could now be appreciated by millions. A joke told on radio instantly entered the public domain, to the dismay of standup comedians everywhere. A big sports event on television was simultaneously viewed by an audience equivalent to a thousand individual arenas. Radio allowed all the family to gather together in the same room and to enjoy the same cultural experience. Television had a similar effect, with "the nuclear family" all watching together in the comfort of their own home.

The thrill felt by every individual who could gain live access to a wide variety of shows, events, and news was only matched by the excitement of politicians and advertisers, who could now gain an immediate connection to those same individuals! Advertising prospered as radio and television provided a cost-efficient mass media platform to promote new products and create powerful consumer brands.

The funds from advertisers allowed broadcasters to bring to a mass audience the best entertainment that money could buy. Programs simply couldn't be missed, and everyone was up to date on the latest turn of events in their favorite shows, and the lives and personalities of featured stars. The availability of electricity and the invention of celluloid film also enabled the magic of cinema. Cinema was another key component of the entertainment industry in the twentieth century. It created "movie stars," Hollywood, and dreams in the minds of millions. Far from being killed by the advent of television, which many had expected, it became a social medium, which allowed friends to go out together and "make a night of it."

The twentieth century really was a golden age for communal, mass entertainment. It was also a golden age for electrical and electronic manufacturers because every home had to have a radio, a television, and a record player right up to the Digital Age. New technology and innovation have delivered a host of ingenious entertainment products over the past 100 years. These products generated ever increasing consumer electronic sales throughout the twentieth century as a result of constant innovation and the demand for in-home and out-of-home entertainment.

Record players that used needles to generate sound waves from vinyl discs played a central role in every home from the 1920s right through to the 1980s. I used to lock myself in my bedroom with my record player and listen to 45 and 33 RPM discs of the Beatles and Rolling Stones at the highest volume my parents would allow. I can remember rushing home from school to watch a program on television and occasionally being allowed to stay up late to see something special. If you ever missed an episode of a popular show, you were sneered at by those who had seen it, and excluded from conversation the next day at school. Television was as integral and important to my life as radio and cinema were to my parents in their past, and the internet is to my daughter today.

A really significant technological breakthrough in the field of consumer electronics was the transistor radio, which delivered wireless portability. The transistor heralded the start of a slew of innovations that increased the number of entertainment devices in the home and out of home. Tape recorders emerged, and then videotapes, both of which allowed consumers to record specific programming and play it later at a time that suited the user. Color televisions gave a massive boost to the television market, just as flat screens and digital sets are still giving it strong support today.

Vinyl records were eventually replaced by CDs using laser technology. Now CDs are disappearing because music can be downloaded from the internet for free or through low-cost subscription services. CD sales declined 20 percent in 2008 in the US, and may become as rare as vinyl records in just a few years. Reel-to-reel tape recorders were supplanted by the eight-track and then the tiny audio cassette. "Ghetto blasters," which were the height of cool just a few years ago were replaced by the Sony Walkman, and it in turn was outmoded by the Apple iPod. Videotapes were replaced first by laserdiscs, then by DVDs. Now streaming video online is endangering the DVD. I wonder how many old vinyl records, videotapes, laserdiscs, and other outmoded forms of entertainment "hardware and software" still exist in the average home? They are rather sad souvenirs of a bygone age, which are now stored in attics and the back of cupboards because we don't want to throw them out for sentimental reasons. They are our personal records of a misspent youth, acne, and changing hormones.

It is amazing that in such a short span of time, so many different entertainment products and even entire categories have soared up the bell curve of acceptance, reached the zenith of mass acceptance, and then plunged down the far side of the curve as a new technology emerged. If you want to study product lifecycles, the consumer electronics arena can probably provide more examples than any other category.

The End of the Giants

Giant new companies were created to cater to the demand for new home entertainment equipment. First in the US with RCA and Zenith, and later in Japan with Sony, Toshiba, Sharp, and Panasonic; and then in Korea with Samsung and LG, and now Chinese companies are emerging. Many consumer electronics companies emerged and then disappeared, usually as a result of being married to a product or technology that became redundant or inadequate in the ever-changing marketplace. For every company that died another took its place, as the market has continued to diversify and innovate. But the Golden Age of Entertainment, in its twentieth-century format, is already in a state of decline.

One-way mass broadcasting is increasingly a thing of the past, and individual interactive entertainment is the future. Network television audiences have been declining inexorably, and have halved over the past 20 years due to the advent of cable and then the internet. Personal selection of shows at a time and place of the individual's choosing has eaten into scheduled television audiences, and will continue to do so.

A 2009 study by media analysis firm Ipsos found that Americans are using the internet to stream more television and movies. This is particularly true of the younger "net natives" who are 18–24 years old. Thirty percent of the group claimed to have streamed a full-length movie over the internet in the past 30 days, revealed the study, and over half had streamed a television show. This was almost double the number from late 2008.

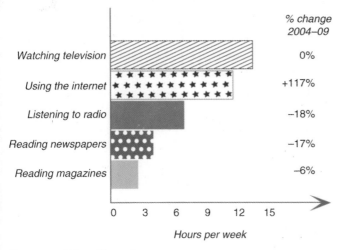

	% change 2004–09
Watching television	0%
Using the internet	+117%
Listening to radio	–18%
Reading newspapers	–17%
Reading magazines	–6%

Hours per week

Figure 2.1 US weekly media usage

In the television era people sat and watched the box, but today people interact and multitask while viewing. Multimedia experience is becoming a normal expectation, and programs are increasingly stretching across television, online, mobile, publishing, music, and videogame arenas. Entertainment is shifting from being a passive occupation to an experiential event.

Young people are spending hours every day with online social networks. They are also developing and sharing their own user-generated content, which is becoming as potent in many ways as that from professional studios. The internet is flooded with home movies, funny real-life videos, and personal diaries. Gamers are spending hours absorbed in their favorite game, or playing with countless others who share their passion. The enormous range of online and mobile entertainment options are already taking up a large part of many people's time, leaving less and less opportunity for watching live television broadcasts and reading print publications (see figure 2.1).

There will still be a huge "content production" industry, with Hollywood and Bollywood as glamorous as ever. But *how* and *when* that content is consumed will continue to evolve. The big studios will have to fight for attention and time in an ever more complex environment, in which consumers are talking, texting, listening, and gaming. Any company in the entertainment industry will need to be highly inventive and move fast to gain share of people's time or wallets in the twenty-first century.

A good example of how the entertainment industry has had to transform its business model is in the music category. From the time that Thomas Edison invented the phonograph in 1877, the music industry made its money from the sale of playable hardware. The hardware was initially prerecorded cylinders, then gramophone discs, and finally compact discs. The music was embossed onto a disc that could be played on a turntable or player. This century old business model has changed over the past few years. Appreciation of music, and demand for music content, has continued to thrive, but the way it is acquired and how it is used has changed dramatically.

The music industry's revenue has fallen precipitously from $14.6 billion in 1999 to $8.5 billion in 2008. The primary reason has been the digitization and downloading of music from the internet, and the ease with which CDs could be bootlegged. Handheld devices are now the primary vehicles for music appreciation as iPods and iPhones enable a user to select and download all his or her personal preferences. So the music industry is in the process of transforming its business model to "licensing," rather than one based on the sale of discs. It has no choice, because trying to stop the spread of computer filesharing is like trying to contain a virus: an almost impossible task once the pandemic has begun. The old hardware sales model, and the CDs that it generated, is heading down the slippery back slope of the bell curve and will ultimately be another casualty of innovation and change in the Digital Age.

There is opportunity for the music industry to create new strategic partnerships with a wide variety of businesses that could open new doors for revenue growth. For example, partnering online music libraries, or taking royalties from new games, or building music accessibility into other entertainment devices, will all enable a viable fee-based business model. Micropayment is one of the key growth areas this century, and the music industry should be a major beneficiary. The $10.99 CD is being replaced by the one-cent download.

The consumer electronics industry has always relied on product innovation to maintain its healthy manufacturing base and profitability. Consumer electronics companies make items and sell them. However, the strength of any entertainment related business in the future will not be in hardware manufacturing, it will be in software development. It will not be in selling manufactured products, it will be in licensing user entertainment applications. This will require most companies in the entertainment sector, including consumer electronics manufacturers, to change their business models quickly.

The Power of Convergence

The reason that so many consumer electronic businesses will become threatened is a keyword for the twenty-first century: *convergence*. Bill

Gates predicted the "teleputer" well over a decade ago, as he anticipated the convergence of the computer and television technology. Bill clearly envisaged products and technologies converging, but entire industries are now converging as a result of the Digital Age. The ways we access communication, entertainment, information, education, and data collection are all converging into a single device. The bigger distinction is now between fixed and mobile devices, rather than information, communication, or entertainment industries.

Convergence means that we can use the same technology to undertake a myriad of different tasks, and access a broad range of disparate facilities. The handheld device that began life as a simple mobile phone just a few years ago has already evolved into a pocket computer providing high speed, online access. In China, almost one-third of all mobile phone users access the internet in this way. The "mobile" in your pocket can already deliver more services than the combination of a television, radio, PC, telephone, CD player, and DVD.

There is still some short-term growth opportunity for television manufacturers, for example, with the sale of flat-screen high-definition televisions as broadcasting goes entirely digital, but this is likely to reach maturity within the next decade. In addition, the promise of 3D is adding a further lifeline to television manufacturers. However, 3D still requires the wearing of special glasses which is inconvenient and uncomfortable. So I can't see the benefit in wearing these spectacles to watch a screen instead of using virtual reality headgear.

The innovation that may take over much of the function of the television is a new generation of tiny projectors entering the market. They are small enough to carry in a pocket or be embedded in a handheld device. These projectors will allow the sharing of photos, charts, websites, or videos, simply by projecting the image onto any convenient wall or flat space. It may soon be possible to project a holographic image that doesn't even need a screen.

Imagine talking to a person who is "virtually" standing in the same room. It's not science fiction, it's happening now. You could watch a movie in a bar with a couple of friends using your mobile device, or make a business presentation in any location. Projectors could be the new technology which finally kills off the television, and they are now just creeping onto the very leading edge of the bell curve.

Newer televisions are more environmentally friendly, use far less power, and provide higher definition, which will incentivize replacement purchases over the near term. Maybe 3D television will offer a new experience to sports fans, and add a further extension to the life of television. However, the television as a heavy, stand-alone, sole provider of entertainment programming will gradually lose out to new projection devices and multifunction "teleputers." Lightweight, flexible screens, or new types of projection facilities, will drive traditional televisions down their maturity curve.

How many homes don't already have a television and a computer? How often will these devices be upgraded? How soon will all television monitors be outmoded by new projection devices? These are all very big questions facing the manufacturers of old fashioned televisions, and for the factories committed to mass producing millions of potentially unwanted sets, and their employees. One thing is certain, if you are still working for a manufacturer of traditional, boxy, analog televisions, you're going to be unemployed very soon. This is a category that is in terminal decline and about to drop off the mature side of the bell curve into oblivion.

The Entertainment Age is morphing into a subset of the Information Age, as the tools and techniques we use to obtain entertainment programming become the same as those we use for education and communication. Perhaps the company most clearly in the eye of the storm is Sony. This powerful, appreciated brand straddles consumer electronics, telephony, film and music production, and gaming. It has, over the years, led different industries and created entirely new categories.

However, every one of the businesses Sony is involved in is undergoing fundamental change. As a result, Sony seems to be unsure whether it is a consumer goods company that provides entertainment software, or an entertainment company that provides consumer goods hardware. However it chooses to define itself, Sony will need to find a way to bring all these disparate strands together in a unique way. If it can't find synergy between all of these diverse assets, then the sum of the parts will not be equal to the whole. Perhaps this is why Sony is now less valued by the stock market than the highly focused Nintendo?

Each of the different parts of Sony's entertainment empire is in an industry that is undergoing transformation. Music and movie delivery systems are being transformed by the ability to download from the internet, and traditional means of program transmission are rapidly being replaced. A completely new revenue model is required by Sony and everyone else in the music and movie supply business. Gaming and the PlayStation have been technologically "outmoded" by Wii, and Sony has failed properly to use in its games the music and movies assets it owns.

Many of Sony's consumer electronics products such as televisions are at the top of their bell curve, or maturing fast and slipping down the far side of the curve. As a result, the categories that Sony is in are becoming commoditized with the entry of possibly hundreds of different brands. The massive supply of new televisions for example far outstrips demand, and the result is declining revenue and profit margins. Sony is essentially an "analog company," which needs to transform itself into the digital world. Fast.

It is a company with a superb record of innovation in a range of consumer goods product categories, many of which were created by Sony itself. But Sony seems to be locked into a linear development and progression within each category, rather than seeking a complete paradigm shift to reinvent the entire company. In a way, Sony epitomizes all the challenges of the entertainment industry and its associated consumer electronics products.

Entertainment has become experiential, integrated, and multimedia. Sony has all the elements to deliver to these needs and dominate the entertainment industry, but it needs to find a unique platform to deliver everything that today's audience wants. Maybe getting into the automobile, or should I say personal transportation vehicle, business isn't such a bad idea for Sony. It has to be a lot easier than consumer electronics and entertainment!

The Digital Age

The digital revolution is far more significant than the invention of writing or even of printing.
—Douglas Engelbart (inventor of the computer mouse)

First, the definition:
- Digitization is the process of converting information into discrete units of data called bits that are usually compiled in multiple-bit groups called bytes. These are the binary data that any device with computing capacity can process.
- Text and images can be digitized by a scanner, which captures an image, including any text, and converts it to a digital file.
- Audio and video digitization uses one of many conversion processes in which an analog signal is changed, without altering its essential content, into a multilevel digital signal.

Digitizing information makes it easier to preserve, access, and share. The Digital Age has revolutionized the way we work, play and communicate. We can now share a document or image with millions of people in just a few seconds. We can store the equivalent of millions of paper pages on a tiny USB stick. We can obtain almost any information we want in moments thanks to digital search engines. We can buy and sell and discuss any topic with people we've never met from all around the world in real time.

The digital revolution is in full swing, and continues to create life-changing innovations almost daily. The core platform that has powered many digital innovations is the internet. The internet has added speed and accessibility to technological innovation.

Social Media

It took 89 years for the wired telephone to gain 150 million users from its invention in 1876 to 1965. Television took 38 years, from 1928 to 1966. Mobile phones took 14 years to achieve the same number of users between 1983 and 1997. The iPod reached this total in just seven years. And Facebook, the social networking site, added its 150 millionth user within just five years from inception. Facebook was adding 50,000 new users per day to its site! (See figure 2.2.)

Communication technologies, and related devices and services, have been rocket propelled with the advent of digital capability. The additional linkage of the internet drove innovation into hyperdrive. I won't even begin to try to predict innovations over the course of this century which the Digital Age will create. Already we're finding that what we can imagine, we can achieve in so many different areas. However,

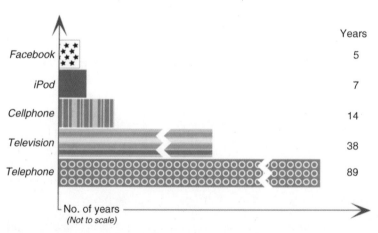

Figure 2.2 Years to reach 150 million users

there is one fundamental driver that will affect much of the new development, and that is the human desire to communicate and interact.

Early users of the telephone assumed it would have limited use as a business tool, and couldn't imagine it being used for social interaction. Similarly, manufacturers of mainframes scoffed at the idea of a computer eventually being in every home. It was after all a business tool not a toy. Both underestimated the fundamental human need to communicate, and the sheer enjoyment that comes from having conversations and sharing experiences with friends and acquaintances.

Human social interaction is a primary mover for a host of categories, and any technology that enables communication and relationship building will thrive. The internet has allowed individuals to participate in a host of local, national, and global communities, and be part of a range of discrete communities with shared needs and interests.

Just as music created a "generation gap" in the mid-twentieth century, social networking sites initially created a similar divergence between young and old. Younger people were far more willing, or eager, to share information about themselves, whereas their parents placed a greater value on privacy. But recent data indicate a significant increase in the use of social network sites by older generations, especially females over 50 years of age. So we can expect baby-boom retirees to stay in touch in this way, and social networking to be widely used across all age profiles.

Other social networks provide communication platforms for people with similar interests, concerns, and activities even if the users don't know who each other are. This "virtual world" involves millions of people, who form communities and interact online. Every evening, for example, millions of online gamers challenge people they have never met in person. In most cases, they don't know their real names or locations. They are complete strangers communicating and enjoying the same interests. We have all watched the same television program at the same time as millions of other people, but we haven't actually talked or interacted with that huge audience. This is possible on the internet.

A game called World of Warcraft has 11.5 million active subscribers. There are battles and entire wars being fought every night around the globe, and we don't even know it! Someone in the entertainment business told me recently that "Gaming is the new Hollywood." And the numbers bear that out: the video game industry is projected to be worth a staggering $68 billion by 2012.

Interestingly, the music tracks of the video games are enjoyed so much that live concerts are now dedicated to playing them. Many of the composers of videogame soundtracks and music are now becoming "rock stars" themselves. And videogames have given "classic" artists such as the Beatles, Aerosmith, and Metallica a host of new fans after being featured on gaming products.

Word of Mouth

Perhaps the biggest danger that the internet holds is that there is an assumption that whatever is online is true. There is a mistaken belief that online opinions are unbiased and that facts are all accurate. The reason for this is the veracity of many websites and the personal nature of most online conversations. For example, Wikipedia has become the encyclopedia of choice, and has completely eclipsed *Encyclopedia Britannica*. Wikipedia has been built by its users. All the entries are created from online submissions.

A key reason for Wikipedia's credibility is that it will indicate whenever a submission doesn't meet its standards, or needs additional input. By flagging this "reader beware" notice, the overall credibility of Wikipedia as *the* source of information and knowledge is increased. This doesn't happen with printed, offline publications.

Other specialist websites do the same thing in their field of activity, so that the trust level of the internet is extremely high. In addition, social network platforms and messaging sites allow people who know each other either directly or indirectly to communicate with sometimes jaw-dropping openness and honesty. So we have a medium that is *more trusted than television or radio*, and it is intensely personal (see figure 2.3).

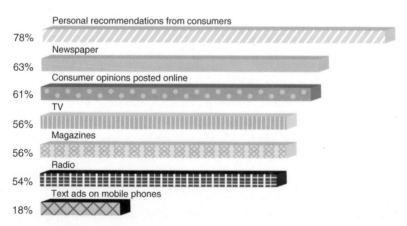

Personal recommendations from consumers

78%

Newspaper

63%

Consumer opinions posted online

61%

TV

56%

Magazines

56%

Radio

54%

Text ads on mobile phones

18%

Figure 2.3 Types of advertising trusted by internet users
Source: The Nielsen Company, "Online Global Consumer Study" press release, October 2007.

The danger is that every opinion and fact is taken at face value and trusted. Online communication is an electronic extension of personal conversations, so although we don't necessarily agree with every opinion, we usually regard it as truthful. Before buying a new product, we usually ask others whether they have tried it and whether they liked it. We weigh up the personal recommendations and very often make a purchase decision largely based on the opinion of others. Marketers know that the most powerful advertising is word of mouth. One personal recommendation is worth a hundred paid ads.

The internet is the most powerful tool for word of mouth recommendations ever conceived.

In the past, word of mouth involved only a few people. Perhaps we discussed an item with just friends or acquaintances while chatting over a cup of coffee, or maybe with some colleagues at work. Now we ask hundreds, thousands, or millions of complete strangers their opinions of a product or service by going online and doing a little research. The internet has become a really powerful influencer of product purchase.

"Consumers are investing more in research before they actually make a purchase. They are taking more time to think it through," says Sara Kleinberg, head of retail marketing at Google.

In some categories 80 percent of people say they go on line to research an item before buying. Entire sites, such as tripadvisor.com, provide a platform for users to share their experiences and give their opinions about hotels, destinations, airlines, restaurants, and many other travel-related topics. And we believe them all! "Surely these people have no reason to lie?" we say to ourselves.

Blogging now affects everything from new products to politics. A new product can be killed before it even gets off the ground by disgruntled users venting their spleen on the internet. A small budget movie can become a blockbuster through online rave reviews. The mere fact that we're sharing the medium of the internet, and specific websites, with other "likeminded" people, leads us to trust them. But the reality is that we do not know them, and in many cases we should not trust them.

Paid bloggers and professional word-of-mouth companies are giving opinions and boosting products or services without identifying themselves. They pretend to be impartial consumers, but are in actuality paid advocates who are employed to "talk up" a brand. More and more marketing funds are being put into online advocacy because it is so potent.

Because of its credibility, the online medium is increasingly being used to create rumor, innuendo, and plain lies. Politicians are seeding false stories online and playing dirty tricks on their opponents. They can say and imply whatever they want, because attribution is not necessary. If enough "rubbish" is thrown, some of it will stick. During the most recent US elections, I received several "factual" messages about Obama being a communist agent, and being in the pocket of left-wing special interests. Not to mention him having a secret agenda to develop Islam in the US . . . Some of the "analyses" exposing Obama's secret agendas were farcical, yet people still circulated them as fact to friends and colleagues.

Disclosures about an online campaign to smear Conservative Party leaders recently caused the resignation of some senior staff employed by the Labor Party in the UK. I read a book recently in which all the action revolved around the seeding of a supposedly smuggled video of someone being tortured in Russia. It created a global crisis and pushed countries towards war because it added "proof" to existing prejudices. The video featured an actor and was designed to ferment conflict between superpowers by manipulating public opinion and creating outrage. It may have been fiction, but I wonder how long it will be before false, manipulative videos do create major real-life problems and conflict?

We all believe that we will recognize genuine comment from paid advocacy, and that we can distinguish between real videos and commercial efforts. This is increasingly untrue, and will become a much bigger issue in the future as online advocacy becomes the primary method of promoting products and special interests.

Open Source Business

The World Wide Web was invented by Tim Berners-Lee in 1989, and over the past 20 years the internet has come to be the dominant global vehicle for communication, information, and entertainment. In comparison to the people who made the Web what it is today, Tim was a relatively old man at age 33 when he first explained and demonstrated his invention.

The early developers of PCs and the software that allowed them to operate, as well as the websites to which they were connected, were mainly in their late teens or twenties. Microsoft, Apple, Google, Yahoo!, YouTube, Facebook, and many other businesses were all created by people under 30 years of age who shared the excitement, emotions, and aspirations of their generation.

IBM, H-P, Apple, Adobe, and the other companies in the computer hardware and software sector could not, and did not, create monster search-engines, information warehouses, news sites, and social networks. Bill Gates and Steve Jobs still do their best to retain their youthful, visionary, and adventurous perspectives that allowed them to create Microsoft and Apple while they were still in their formative years. But little by little, many high-tech companies are becoming more reliant on traditional business models, and innovation is purchased rather than created.

Staying in touch with the aspirations and emotional needs of web users and being less obsessed with technology and functionality for its own sake will be critical to all high-tech companies. The "build it and they will come" business model has proved successful for the Web itself and many websites and related product innovations. But providing new technology simply because it is possible to do so will result in failure if it is not designed to satisfy specific consumer needs.

Most IT and telecoms companies are led by older generations who remain wedded to existing communications models and are driven primarily by new functionality. They need to be more consumer-centric, and deliver to human needs, rather than simply drive technological progress for its own sake. This may require a change in the product development process of many high-tech companies, which may find that they can create more successful products by sharing their plans publicly and encouraging input from prospective consumers. This type of "open-source" product development may be the savior of high-tech companies, as they allow their users to play an integral role in product development. Essentially, the role of the company becomes being manager and project leader, as innovation and fresh ideas come up from their enormous user base or the internet.

Product development and innovation becomes bottom up driven, not top down. Many websites allow their users to adapt and change a site to meet their needs. Even the best platforms accede to their users' requests. The most celebrated example of this was the Facebook revolution in 2006. The website introduced a new feature called "news feeds," which communicated personal information about users to the homepages of all their friends. It changed the nature of the website, and its users weren't at all happy. So within a few days 750,000 Facebook users banded together to demand changes to the privacy aspects of the site. Facebook listened and rapidly made the changes to meet its users' needs and keep them loyal.

How many companies have the ability to do this? Could a car company make changes to its designs before the vehicle actually hits the road? Could a computer or mobile phone company immediately change design or functionality if its users weren't happy with the product? Rapid, consumer-led changes and innovations will be an increasing feature of the

Digital Age. Companies may need to change to user-driven, open-source operations, as the market situation changes so rapidly.

Many companies are communicating with individual clients to deliver customized products. A recent survey indicated that 40 percent of companies already provide some sort of product customization, and most expected to be doing so in the very near future. The internet is making customization easier. Various e-commerce sites already allow you to design your own running shoes, jeans, and shirts, or personalize your car, candy packaging, and various containers.

Customer collaboration is practiced by many companies as they seek ideas and then allow their buyers to vote on the implementation of the best ones. Perhaps the role model for many companies is Tim Berners-Lee himself, who made his idea freely available, with no patents or royalties. The World Wide Web Consortium, which he founded, decided that its standards should be based on royalty-free technology, so that they could easily be adopted by anyone. This allowed the rapid development of the Web and its associated sites, and empowered anyone to get involved without charge.

Telecommunications Convergence

The internet has enabled communications over a *free* global platform, which is increasingly threatening the business model of telecoms companies. In addition, the rapid convergence of technology is jeopardizing the future of many companies in the communications and related sectors.

The mobile phone has evolved from being a large "brick" with poor reception, to a small, extremely sophisticated communication and imaging device. However, with the addition of internet connectability, and a wave of new applications, "phones" are evolving into all-in-one, multi-purpose handheld devices. These new handheld devices will provide a complete suite of communication, information, entertainment, imaging, and financial facilities.

The primary function of a handphone is rapidly becoming the provision of internet access, rather than oral communication. Soon it will also become the simplest way to buy goods, pay bills, carry tickets, and provide proof of purchase. Already in Japan you can pay utility bills with your phone, or buy various items from high-tech vending machines, and make a variety of other payments. The handphone isn't replacing the credit card, but it may soon take over many of its features. Japanese cellphone users can also obtain coupons and other benefits by using Quick-Response codes (your camera takes a picture of the code on an ad or poster and automatically takes you to the website, or downloads information).

Airlines are sending boarding passes to your handphone, and you simply run the code displayed on the screen over a scanner at the gate to board. Phones already have street directories and guides to cities where you live or are visiting. Handheld devices will become even more indispensable than they already are as the century progresses. This convergence of technologies into a single mobile device is bringing computer, cellphone, and telecoms companies into a mixture of alliances and collision courses.

Apple jumped ahead of the phone manufacturers with its iPhone, but within a year Nokia, Samsung, Sony Ericsson, and others had similar devices. Computer companies are now creating handheld devices, as are phone companies. Both are in a convergence race to provide a handheld device that has almost every conceivable application. And consumers are lapping it up.

There is a real desire to have a single personal communications device that can provide voice, video, and written communication, plus accessing, recording, and playing still and moving images on demand. With our handheld device, we can access almost anything, and be as accessible as we choose. Barack Obama famously refused to be separated from his BlackBerry. He was addicted to "staying in touch," just like the rest of us.

Losing your mobile phone is a disaster for most people. You lose immediate contact with your world and lifestyle. Taking away your son or daughter's cellphone for a day is a punishment that should only be meted out for the worst of offences!

In the near future, all simple oral calls will be made by VOIP, which uses the internet connection itself, rather than a separate telephone line. Calls will therefore be free. Free connectivity from mobile devices using VOIP has already begun, and will continue to climb the bell curve of acceptance to become the dominant voice communication medium.

Although line charges have rapidly declined, the cost of calls and SMSs still account for a very large proportion of young people's disposable income, and are a sizable expense for business. So users will take every opportunity to eliminate those charges. This will require telecoms companies to develop a new revenue model as call-charges based on time, distance, and duration will eventually evaporate.

The telephone is a 100-year-old technology. It's time for a change. Charging for phone calls is something you did last century.
—Niklas Zennstrom (founding partner of Skype)

Telecoms and cellphone and all high-tech companies need to be very clear about their core competences, and what services they wish to provide in a rapidly changing marketplace.

The computer manufacturer Apple has already "crossed over" to become the most leading-edge digital phone company with its iPhone. Dell is reported to be introducing a "smart phone" in China soon. Already we have strategic alliances that bring technological expertise together. What other corporate and brand crossovers, partnerships, or transformations will occur in the race for convergence?

For those businesses that remain in the computer hardware and software category, their margins will continue to be eroded if all they do is focus on manufacturing efficiency or better distribution. The category thrives on innovation, and without consistent new product development, hardware manufacturers wither and die. Who remembers Atari, Wang, DEC, Prime, NeXT, and Commodore? Once they were big, powerful companies, but died because they either failed to change their business model, or failed to innovate quickly enough.

One high-tech company that has completely transformed itself is IBM. Here is a company that was highly dependent on mainframe computers, and its business model was based on the sale or lease of hardware and the provision of computing services to business. It was also the leading manufacturer of electric typewriters. How did this manufacturer of two products that were about to be decimated by PCs survive? IBM completely transformed itself from a supplier of computer hardware into a new consulting and analytics business.

It sold its typewriter division, then its PC business, and got out of the disk-drive business. IBM used the cash from those sales to buy more than 100 companies that fitted with its new vision, including Pricewater-houseCoopers Consulting. Spending more than $50 billion on new acquisitions, it made the strategic shift from being a computer manufacturer to a high-level consulting business with extraordinarily good profit margins. In 2008, IBM reported $103 billion of revenue, with a 44 percent profit margin. Most companies and their CEOs would kill for those kind of numbers!

Compare IBM with its mainframe competitors from the past: Univac, Burroughs, and ICL, all are effectively dead and buried. It required "best of breed" CEOs to make the IBM transformation happen, and only then with considerable angst and pain. The transition to a new business model requires foresight and an unswerving commitment to change that not many companies can deliver. Look at the current PC manufacturers all struggling to compete in an increasingly commoditized marketplace. Their sole objective is to try to be the low-cost provider despite incurring consistently lower margins. One by one, they will gradually go out of business unless they can find new opportunities or change their business model.

> *The digital business is a fantastic business to be in. The only thing you have to do is build a cost structure for a declining business, which is different from the structure for a growing business.*
> —Antonio Perez, CEO, Kodak

Digital Print

Another segment of the communications industry facing the need to undergo a complete business transformation to the Digital Age is printing and publishing. The key issue for newspapers, magazines and book publishers is that they need to find a way to monetize their digital content. They have rushed into providing online versions of their publications, but very few have been able to gain subscriber fees in the same way as selling "hard" copies. The internet medium itself is seen as providing "free" access to information, so there is a natural disinclination to paying for content. Only publishers of "need to know" information have had any success, such as the *Wall Street Journal*, *The Economist*, or *Harvard Business Review*.

The advent of the portable "electronic reader" or "e-reader" is most likely to be the technological breakthrough that will enable business model transformation for publishers. The Kindle reader is the best of a new generation of portable, handheld, reading "slates," to which published material can be sent. At present, Amazon.com is the primary developer of a new sales process by which electronic copies of a book (e-book) can be purchased and transmitted to the Kindle electronic reader. The cost of an e-book is considerably less than the price of a traditionally published paper book. And it is a lot more environmentally friendly. No trees need to be cut down to read an e-book. No printing, no ink, and no expensive, weighty, delivery.

E-readers use a new type of "electronic ink" on a sharp white screen to provide the same sort of experience as reading on traditional paper. The promise of e-readers is very exciting. They will be light and flexible for easy portability and use, and be able to download newspapers and magazines to which you have subscribed wirelessly and automatically.

Turn the pages with a simple push of a button, or choose to flip a page, as you do with an iPhone.

E-readers won't just provide fast, easy, low-cost, portable publishing, they will also open up a new era of interactivity. A user could see an ad or article of interest and use the wireless or internet connection to request more information or view a demo video, or go to a related website.

Most excitingly for publishers, readers can buy and download an e-book, and then share their thoughts about the book with others who have read it. They can join e-reader book clubs and become fully involved with others who have similar interests or enjoy reading books by the same authors. Authors themselves can get to know their readers, and what they like and don't like about their books. E-readers will even allow you to go to a dictionary to look up a word you don't know, or to Wikipedia to get more information on someone or something you've been reading about.

A key benefit for users of e-readers will be lower cost. Because there is no need to print the publications, buyers will expect, and get, lower prices. This will reduce revenue to publishers for each newspaper, magazine, or book, but lower cost and easier purchasing should increase volumes and sustain income levels. This will work in the same way that the music industry moved from selling expensive CDs to "leasing" downloadable music. Publishers will have to move away from selling printed documents to transmitting "content" for a lower price.

Ease of access and lower cost usually result in greater sales. E-readers will also throw up all kinds of new opportunities. The electronic format allows such innovations as "read the first chapter free," and if you like it, then buy the book: a kind of in-depth, electronic-bookstore, browsing facility. Or books could be sold by the chapter or episode, just as Charles Dickens and many other Victorian authors did in their day to generate greater sales. The cost of a single episode was affordable by virtually everyone, and excitement (and greater sales) was built by leaving every episode with a "cliffhanger" ending, which readers would talk about while they anticipated the next episode! Readers who joined later could simply purchase the back copies.

Newspaper, magazine and book sales could well increase significantly by using some of these techniques that the e-reader provides, and the lower product cost. However, I suspect that most newspaper and magazine publishers will need to redefine their business, and possibly undergo significant transformation. For a start they won't be "publishers" any more, they will be content providers. They will need to define very carefully what content they will generate themselves versus what they will acquire from global news services (such as Reuters, AP, and UPI) and freelance writers or reporters.

The core skills of a newspaper or magazine will increasingly be focused on editing, content management, negotiation of distribution rights, and promotion of the brand and its values. Newspapers and magazines will employ far fewer reporters and correspondents, and rely more and more on outsourced news and content providers. Newspapers may become more like movie studios, which have a small core staff who commission new productions, line up distribution, and generate publicity. The actual movie content is provided by independent contractors, who conceive the movie, which the studio underwrites. In other cases, independent producers shoot a movie, then sell their completed work to the studio. The studios gain their revenue by distributing and promoting the movies through a variety of channels.

This same process of getting revenue from distributor sales may form the basis of publishers' business models in the future. Revenue streams may well come from phone suppliers who offer newspaper distribution to an e-reader as one of their caller package options. The phone company will then share its additional subscriber revenue with the publication. "Deadlines" will become less relevant because distribution will be instant and not require any printing presses or delivery vans to rush around town in the early hours of the morning.

Subscribers will likely expect "breaking news" to be transmitted to them as it occurs, and not have to wait for the daily delivery of the newspaper. Newspapers could compete more effectively with television for real-time news, as newsflashes go to the phone, and full content to the e-reader. So in the near future, Verizon or T-Mobile may become the biggest "publishers" of newspapers and magazines, and the *New York Times* or the *Daily Telegraph* will evolve into branded news content "bureaus" of just 20 or 30 people, who filter and format content for their particular subscriber-group needs. Any actual paper publishing would be outsourced to a separate printing business, which would face increasing criticism by environmentalists!

By the way, if you're already reading this on a Kindle, I'm proud of you!

3 Global Branding

It is not the employer who pays the wages.
Employers only handle the money. It is the
customer who pays the wages.

—Henry Ford

The Industrial Revolution created goods in mass quantities at prices that were affordable to a large proportion of the population. Thus mass consumption was born and has continued to grow throughout the past 200 years and more.

The advent of household electricity and the power of carbon fuel burning engines combined both to create and to generate demand for a plethora of new consumer products. These innovative new products generated entire "Ages" as has already been noted, as their mass appeal spawned entire new industries based on the production of a wide variety of global brands.

Huge multinational corporations were built that catered to accelerating consumer demand in country after country. First they were British, such as Dunlop, Cunard, Rolls-Royce, Lever, Shell, and Cadbury. Then American, with Coca-Cola, Gillette, Ford, P&G, Hoover, Disney, J&J, Xerox, IBM, McDonald's, Microsoft, and Starbucks. European multinational corporations include Mercedes, Nestlé, Bayer, BMW, Dior, Moët, Louis Vuitton, and Zara. Japan gave us the omnipresent Sony, Toyota, Panasonic, Toshiba, Mitsubishi, and Nissan. Most recently, Korea has created some powerful global brands including LG, Samsung, Daewoo, and Hyundai, and the next to emerge will be Chinese and Indian multinationals.

These giant corporations succeeded by developing and effectively marketing new products that met burgeoning consumer needs. Equally important, those consumer needs were based on surprisingly homogenous attitudes and values. A key feature of the twentieth century was "the global village," postulated by Marshall McLuhan. The recognition that a more homogenous consumer was emerging globally, was thanks largely to the medium of television.

A middle-class television-watching consumer in Mumbai had far more in common with his or her counterpart in Minneapolis or Mainz or Melbourne, than with a rural farmer in his or her own country who had barely enough to live on. Middle-class consumers spanned the globe and had surprisingly similar aspirations and attitudes. McLuhan postulated that one reason may be that the medium itself was the message. When a family had enough money to afford a television, the medium changed the user's lifestyle regardless of the message.

Television was therefore a prime mover in providing entry into a world of privilege and consumption, and a lifestyle with a more intense desire for consumer goods and their benefits. The aspirations of young Vietnamese families watching television today are fundamentally no different than those of young Americans whose eyes were glued to the "box" 50 years ago.

The hundreds of millions (yes, hundreds of millions) of Chinese and Indians who became serious consumers over the past two decades wanted the same lifestyle and goods that Europeans and Americans acquired earlier in the century. And they want them now!

I saw how rapidly Asian markets developed over the past two decades when marketers were forced by consumer demand to "leapfrog" product development to provide the latest designs and functionality. Spending considerable time in China in the 1980s and 1990s, I was staggered at the speed of change and the ready acceptance of new products and technology. For example, most Chinese consumers went from having no phones at all to becoming one of the fastest-growing, most-developed cellphone nations in the world. They simply missed out on fixed-line telephone networks, which were expensive and too slow to build. They also went from washing their hair with hand soap, to 2-in-1 shampoos and even 3-in-1 shampoos in the space of a year or two. The gradual adoption of shampoo and a basic understanding of its different functions were overwhelmed by the rush into the most leading-edge products.

It was the same in category after category. The Chinese consumer adopted new products at a speed that was breathtaking, and clearly showed how quickly change can occur with latent demand for a better quality of life. The country changed from a communist ethos to a raging, unfettered capitalism. We called China "the Wild East," because there were no rules, and everyone grabbed as much as they could for themselves. The economy exploded as the innate business savvy of the Chinese was fueled by massive financial support and foreign investment. The desire to improve their standard of living and acquire the trappings of affluence that had taken half a century or more to accumulate in other parts of the world took only a single generation in China to grow.

Because of all these new consumers, it is tempting to think that there will be an ever-increasing demand for the same type of consumer goods. More consumers should mean greater demand. Higher incomes should equal increased volumes. This may be true in emerging markets around the world, especially in Asia, where there is still a fundamental desire to acquire "basic" consumer goods like cars and computers that newly affluent families don't yet have. But in the developed world, where consumer goods are regarded as standard equipment, fundamental changes in attitude are occurring. These will become global shifts as the century progresses, and include every country as it economically matures.

Several factors are now combining to create a new "post-consumer" society in the twenty-first century. This doesn't mean that people won't continue to consume, but *what* they consume, *why* they consume, and *how much* they consume will definitely change. Various factors are contributing to this change. Some are demographic, some attitudinal, and others economic, but they are all combining to create a major behavioral shift, which will effect massive changes in consumption patterns. Multinational companies will find it is a much more difficult environment in which to build and sustain global brands.

4

The Consumer Century

The twentieth century saw many countries around the world change into postindustrial societies driven by consumerism and conspicuous consumption. As the century progressed, country after country saw its national GDP growth, tax income, and corporate revenues all become underpinned by aggressive, growing consumerism.

Affluence bred the aspiration for bigger, better lifestyles, and created an ever-stronger need for self-esteem and recognition. New technology enabled the creation and mass production of an enormous range of products that catered to this consumer demand. The interests of government, companies, and affluent buyers combined into a single overwhelmingly powerful Consumer Century.

The strongest global economic driver in the late twentieth century was consumerism, which was powered by the human aspiration for self-esteem and the values that drove that behavior. The term "conspicuous consumption" was first used by an economist called Thorsten Veblen in a book published in 1899. *The Theory of the Leisure Class* heralded the start of the Consumer Century by describing the behavioral characteristics of an emerging "nouveau riche" class of people. In the course of the nineteenth century a second Industrial Revolution had emerged, which created mass employment and delivered regular compensation to employees. Salaried employment generated new wealth and a greater individual ability to purchase goods. Veblen focused his attention on the upper class and noted how they used their economic wealth to exercise social power. This social power, he noted, may be real or simply perceived as a result of conspicuous consumption. He observed the irrational and unnecessary purchase of goods simply to attain status.

Veblen noted that "people will undergo a very considerable degree of privation in the comforts or the necessaries of life in order to afford what is considered a decent amount of wasteful consumption; so that it is by no means an uncommon occurrence, in an inclement climate, for people to go ill clad in order to appear well dressed."

He had great difficulty understanding why people would buy things for hedonistic or narcissistic reasons. It seemed so illogical, and contrary to conventional economic theory. Veblen was also a sociologist, and was both amazed and amused as he observed the actions that humans took to increase their own sense of self-worth once they had sufficient disposable income to do so. When an even broader, wealthier middle class emerged in the twentieth century, the expression "conspicuous consumption" began to be applied to the actions of any person or household that purchased goods primarily to display their new-found affluence and status. As Veblen had earlier noted, the actual quality and utility of the goods purchased were often of far less importance than the social status they communicated and the envy they created.

Consumerism and conspicuous consumption played an ever greater role in the twentieth century as wealth increased and the desire to display one's success and status increased. The availability of credit cards and easy loans for household goods, cars, and homes added further impetus to consumption. People learned that they could buy now and pay later. The average American home, for example, based its financial planning on the size of the installments it needed to pay after purchasing an item. Many Americans perceived the price of consumer goods in the context of monthly payments rather than absolute cost. American society and its consumption patterns were based on cash flow, not savings or wealth.

As the twentieth century progressed, any vestige of frugality or saving up to buy something disappeared in an orgy of instant gratification and immediate access. No product was too expensive, and the financial ability to purchase almost anything became available to pretty much everyone in America, and many other developed countries.

Consumer Behavior

Aggressive consumerism occurs whenever a society has developed a reliable currency for trading, and an after-tax income that exceeds the demands of the basic necessities of life—food, drink, accommodation, and clothing. These excess funds, or disposable income, are partly saved and partly used to purchase non-necessities. Non-necessities usually feed the ego, provide pleasure, generate excitement, project self-worth, and generally add to one's sense of wellbeing. For example, a car is regarded as a necessity in many countries, but the selection of the brand and model is inextricably connected to one's sense of style and self-worth. A car is a vehicle (if you'll pardon the pun) for projecting your personality and social standing.

New shoes are rarely purchased by young women with pedestrian functionality entirely in mind. Form and fashion usually count for a lot more than function and fit. Clothing isn't purchased merely to cover one's nakedness and provide warmth. It is again a way to project personality, style and status. "Clothes maketh the man. Naked people have little or no influence on society," noted Mark Twain.

As disposable income rises, the ability and desire to purchase more goods and services follow a similar trend. It allows us to buy more items for pleasure and entertainment rather than necessity, and to enjoy a lifestyle that brings greater satisfaction and more interesting experiences. Real disposable income doubled in most developed markets between 1970 and 1999, and the result was a significant expansion of the retail trade as it provided the goods that more affluent consumers demanded. New fashion stores sprang up on every street, and appliance retailers seemed to dominate many shopping malls.

Over the past 10 years China, India, and many other Asian nations have enjoyed rapid increases in disposable income, often running into double digits per quarter. Again the effects have been quite dramatic, as seen by the construction of countless shopping malls and new consumer outlets.

British and Chinese Consumerism

Mass consumerism has its roots in the Industrial Revolution of the nineteenth century. The employment of a huge number of workers who were paid regular salaries created wealth that gradually percolated throughout society in country after country. Britain was already described by Napoleon as "a nation of shopkeepers" more than 200 years ago, as it developed a huge retail trade pandering to the new affluence that had been created by industry and mass production.

A century of British colonial expansion was driven by the need to develop a secure global network of trading posts for the export of its manufactured products and the import of new luxuries to satisfy consumer demand in a newly affluent home market. Wars were fought over raw materials rather than religion. Tea and rubber, iron ore, and copper were the cause of many conflicts, rather than religion, heredity, and geography as in the past.

By the end of the nineteenth century, Britons and many other nationalities could enjoy the fruits of a true global free-trade environment, and satisfy their every consumer need. Countries that had enjoyed a century of industrial and manufacturing activity, and a network of safe global trading routes, entered the twentieth century with an affluent population ready to start consuming with a vengeance.

It is interesting to note that China is currently following a remarkably similar economic, foreign policy, and military path today to that of Britain 150 years ago. China's economy is driven by the mass production and export of goods to meet growing global demand, just as Britain's was in the nineteenth century. China's foreign policy and investment strategy is driven by the need to secure the reliable supply of the raw materials that its manufacturers need, just as Britain's was throughout the 1800s. And fascinatingly China is increasingly turning to Africa, South America, and Australia as a source of those materials . . . just as Britain did.

Plus ça change, plus c'est la même chose!

Raw material dependency is the reason that China may find itself at political odds with the Western world. The increasing economic interdependence of China with the US and Western Europe has been based on the supply of manufactured goods. So politically China will continue to do whatever is necessary to secure raw materials, even if this means doing deals with the devil. The Sudanese government is being charged with genocide, but China continues to support it, and provide political protection, because it has oil and other strategic minerals. Korea and Iran find a similar protective Chinese umbrella, as do a host of rogue states in Africa, Asia, and Latin America that are mineral rich. So despite a shift to greater global consensus and common values, the Chinese government will buck any trend to deliver the materials its manufacturers need to maintain economic growth.

Perhaps only after China's ticking population time bomb implodes and the country's population begins to decline will we see its foreign policy begin to change, just as Britain's did in the 1900s as it moved toward a postindustrial economy. In the meanwhile, China will continue to try to acquire publicly listed mining and oil companies, and develop joint ventures to gain access to minerals across the world.

In the nineteenth century, Britain acquired a chain of naval ports to provide the safe haven and supplies for its vessels, and to control strategic points across vital trade routes: Gibraltar, Malta, Aden, Colombo, Penang, Singapore, and Hong Kong were one such chain from the UK to the Far East. In the twenty-first century, we can expect to see a massive expansion of China's naval power, both merchant and military. I would not be at all surprised to see the establishment of military bases along trade routes or in key supply markets, and the purchase of port and airport facilities in various mineral-rich countries. China needs to secure its access to minerals and keep its trade routes open, as Britain did in the past. China will also develop alliances with various countries in Asia, Africa and Latin America to protect its access to raw materials and provide military protection to its key corporations if necessary.

Britain's foreign policy very much followed the interests of the East India Company and the Hudson Bay Company in the eighteenth century, and subsequently its huge base of manufacturers and mass producers in the industrialized nineteenth century. We can therefore expect China's foreign policy to go hand in hand with the interests of its major corporations, just as Britain's did in the 1800s.

Manufacturers have become increasingly inclined to move their factories to places where adequate labor exists and costs are lowest. In the past, this sometimes resulted in factories moving to a new location within a given country. However, over the course of the twentieth century, this increasingly meant relocating a factory to another country that offered lower costs, stable government, and hardworking people. Many businesses in developed countries chose to relocate their factories to or source goods from Asian countries, which had the added benefit of significant domestic demand. So Asia, and China in particular, is undergoing an industrial "revolution" as its economies grow rapidly thanks to the manufacturing sector and the export of goods.

The Role of Women

Consumerism is powered by increasing affluence, new aspirations, a growing population, and perhaps most intriguingly, by the entrance of women into the workforce. In the US, only 20 percent of women worked back in the 1920s and 1930s. The war years drew many women into the workforce as necessary replacements for men who were absent in the armed forces. Women subsequently became increasingly accepted into the workforce and took on broader roles in every kind of business. This trend has accelerated strongly, and today over 60 percent of working-age women are now employed in the US, which is twice as many as in the 1950s. At the same time, the number of working men has dropped, so that today almost half of the American workforce is female (see figure 4.1).

Similar trends can be seen in the UK and many other Western countries. Women also make up an enormous proportion of the work-forces in China and India, contributing to their powerful economic growth. Some countries have maintained more traditional roles for women as primarily homemakers, and in Japan, Germany, and Italy women still account for less than 40 percent of the workforce. Given the population decline that these countries are now suffering, as we will discuss later, more working women could add a real shot in the arm to the economy.

Various sources estimate that women generate about 40 percent of global GDP. Women have traditionally been the household shoppers and they are the primary purchasers of household goods. In addition, women buy a huge proportion of all other consumer goods, from clothing to accessories and mobile phones to cosmetics, for their own needs and

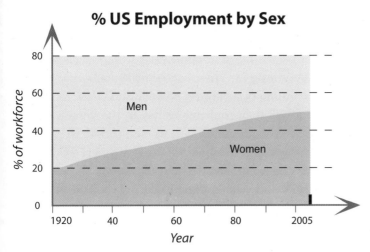

Figure 4.1 US employment by sex

pleasure. If we combine these two roles of household and personal shopper, it adds up to about 80 percent of the volume of all consumer goods bought in most developed countries. And this doesn't include the influence that women have in what has been traditionally the man's domain of cars and holidays.

The freedom that working women enjoy, by earning their own salary and being able to spend their own money, has given consumerism a depth and breadth that men could never have developed alone. The giant industries now devoted to delivering products catering to females are testament to the immense purchasing power wielded by women. A woman's never-ending search for beauty has spawned and developed businesses from the sensible to the truly bizarre, but it has all contributed to the twentieth-century consumerism.

In the UK, there is clear evidence that females achieve better academic results than males, and are perhaps better suited to the types of technical, medical, and service industry that will dominate developed countries in the twenty-first century. So all the signs point to women having better-paying jobs than men in the future and coming to represent a larger proportion of the workforce than males in some countries. But are women any happier now that they can work on the same terms as men? Or is there an increasing depression and unhappiness among many who are failing to balance their careers with family life?

The work–life balance is an issue for both sexes, but is particularly difficult for women and their pivotal role within the family unit. Despite all the business and career opportunities that women have available to them in this new century, it may well be that their pursuit of happiness starts to become far more important than their desire to be driven by career. The measure of joy within their family may well be seen to be far more important than their income. There can be little doubt that women will continue to drive consumption patterns and maintain their role as the primary consumers. But will they continue to buy in the same way, and with the same abandon in the future? Or will women choose to purchase goods in a more considered and value-oriented manner? Will their attitudes and behavior change as broader considerations become more important in their lives? Will women be the leaders of the Age of Selfish Altruism or its victims?

Consumer Spending

As the twentieth century progressed, country after country reached levels of affluence that created eager consumers and equally keen retailers and manufacturers dedicated to meeting their needs. Larger and more elaborate shopping malls sprouted across the world as retailers catered to the broad range of consumer desires. More and more consumer brands emerged to feed the ever more voracious appetite for new products that fed the ego and brought lifestyle pleasure.

In Singapore every family aspires to the 5 Cs: Cash, Credit Card, Condo, Car, and Club. This aspiration is embedded in the national psyche and will probably never change because almost every couple enters marriage with this dream of the future, which is shared by millions of others around Asia and the world. Professor Armin Falk at Bonn University examined brain activity among various subjects in relation to *perceived* wealth. He wanted to find out if brain activity is actually increased by the prospect of higher income. His studies revealed that there is a "money illusion" when people believe that they can buy a lot more with the money they have earned.

The greater the amount of money consumers have access to, the more excited and inclined they are to buy, even if their actual purchasing power is less. For example, people felt "richer" getting a 5 percent pay raise in an environment of 4 percent inflation than a 2 percent pay raise in zero inflation. The study indicates that even thinking about cash stimulates the reward centers in the brain that are involved with pleasure. This suggests that humans are innately susceptible to the illusion of wealth that an increase in financial availability can bring. When they feel wealthier, they are much more inclined to buy.

The Credit Boom

So the massive availability of credit that was a feature of the second half of the twentieth century unleashed a wave of consumerism that turned into a tsunami of spending as consumers felt increasingly affluent. Even if this was not actually true!

Banks have been issuing credit cards for the past 50 years with innovative features and greater flexibility. All of which were designed to stimulate spending, and to make the buying process easier and more rewarding. Providing that you retained a good payment record, the more you spent, the higher your credit limit would go. Credit cards have been the fuel for consumer spending and provided the means to satisfy immediate purchase desires. In the process they eroded thrift as a virtue, and the idea of "saving up" to buy an item became regarded as a strange anachronism.

Banks and finance companies also offered a range of loans to help you buy cars, and hire-purchase arrangements to make the acquisition of fridges, televisions, washing machines, and furniture "more affordable." This allowed consumers to buy whatever they wanted, whenever they wanted. Easy credit created a consumer nirvana. The result was that total consumer debt in America grew from $355 billion in 1980 to a staggering $1.7 trillion by 2001.

In the following seven years, American consumers excelled themselves and added almost another $1 trillion to the size of their debt. US consumer debt by 2008 was approximately $2,700,000,000,000. While supersmart bankers produced ever more inventive credit facilities, a prodigious output of MBAs provided the marketing techniques for a concerted assault on the consumer. An MBA was a passport to a great job, and evidence that you had the discipline and brains to drive business. I won't go into the pros and cons of MBAs as employees, because the successful application of academic theory into a dynamic, real-time business environment is not guaranteed. In my own experience, the MBAs who did well would have done so without the extra qualifications. And MBA failures would have been failures anyway as a result of inadequate personality traits and interpersonal skills, regardless of their academic knowledge. However, regardless of the merits of an MBA, the sheer volume of marketing-savvy professionals produced ensured that companies would remain consumer focused and growth oriented.

The only reason a great many American families don't own an elephant is that they have never been offered an elephant for a dollar down and easy weekly payments.
—Mad magazine

The Role of Advertising

Retailing prospered. Manufacturing delivered. Advertising thrived. My own chosen profession was advertising, which was a great industry for a young person to be in throughout the twentieth century. The ad biz grew exponentially with consumer demand and the increasing number of companies producing new and exciting products that required introduction and development. These ranged from household goods that made housework easier to different modes of transportation; and from an almost uncountable number of new foods and beverages to branded drugs and health products.

The companies that I have worked with include Nestlé, Unilever, DeBeers, Kodak, Kellogg's, Kraft, Ford, Pepsi, Citibank, IBM, Rolex, Burger King, J&J, and a host of airlines, beers and other alcoholic beverages, local retailers, and government agencies.

Did advertising drive excessive consumption? Did it encourage people to buy what they didn't need? Did it only focus on the benefits of a product? Yes, of course it did! Advertising is meant to promote a brand, and to encourage the desire to purchase. It's up to consumers to exercise discretion. And most do. Relatively few people drive themselves into serious debt buying totally unnecessary items. It is usually the house or the car that is repossessed, not the new dress or the special coffee made from monkey droppings. Also, people only buy a bad product once. If it doesn't work, or it isn't useful, it won't be bought again.

However, it is true that many people allowed themselves to be seduced into significant credit card debt in the frenzy of conspicuous consumption that instant accessibility provided. And I confess that I played my part in that.

The past decade has perhaps seen the final explosion of consumer spending, and the absolute zenith of conspicuous consumption. Perhaps even the end of mindless consumerism. By 1989, the average US household was carrying $42,000 of debt, including bank cards, phone cards, and credit cards issued by oil companies and retail stores, mortgages, car loans, and other loans.

In real dollar terms, this had increased 130 percent to $97,000 just 18 years later in 2007. Most of this increase has occurred in the first years of the new millennium, as household debt increased by 52 percent between 2001 and 2007 alone, and almost all of this recent increase was related to mortgages and home-equity loans. The crazy peak of credit facilitation was reached recently when unemployed people in the US were being given $1 million mortgages to buy the house of their dreams. Finally, the illusion of wealth was shattered when repayment was actually required.

Home repossessions, consumer bankruptcies, and business Chapter 11 filings have soared, and spared almost no aspect of American society. Chinese, Japanese, and other foreign and domestic manufacturers that had been supported by American debt suddenly found their sales slumping massively. Does this signal the end of an era? Is it really the beginning of the end of consumerism, and will it herald a more prudent post-consumer society?

Recent data show American savings rates rising to their highest levels for many years. Corporate health is improving, but consumer spending remains soft. Are Americans and the developed world returning to more thrifty ways and entering a new post-consumer society?

During the second half of the twentieth century, the world thrived on a competitive spirit, powered by increasing affluence and easy credit facilities. Consumer-driven societies were dedicated to obtaining goods and belongings that increased their self-esteem and marked their status in society.

The more economically developed a country became, the more thrift was set aside and debt accumulated. By the beginning of the twenty-first century, Americans actually had a negative savings rate. For the first time in history we saw an entire country living off credit to feed its consumerism. "Greed is good" became a mantra for yuppies. "He who dies with the most toys wins!" was the T-shirt motto that probably best sums up the Consumer Century. "A symbol of your success" was the claim on a multitude of advertisements. These attitudes are now changing, and the result will be very different T-shirts and advertising slogans.

Consumer Values

It is easy to define the past Consumer Century by human behavior and the products that were purchased. What are harder to define are the *values* that created the Consumer Century. What were the underlying beliefs, attitudes and desires that melded into a set of values that drove consumerism? The value system of a consumer is what affects his or her purchase behavior.

Every new century has the seeds of its value system sown in the preceding century. To understand twentieth-century values, we need to look back at the nineteenth century.

Nineteenth-Century Values

The nineteenth century was a time of massive attitudinal change, particularly in Britain, which was the leading-edge country for most of the century. Britain was the home of the Industrial Revolution and the creation of a powerful banking industry with credit facilities and a reliable currency. Country after country emulated Britain's transition from a rural, agricultural country to an urban, industrialized state. This created population upheaval as people flocked from the countryside to find work and new opportunity in the new cities.

Manchester, Birmingham, and Glasgow expanded massively in the same way that Shanghai, Manila, Jakarta, Mumbai, Sao Paulo, and Mexico City did a century later. The rural poor always dream of work in the city that will give them a reliable salary. However, many dreams were shattered in the slums of nineteenth-century Birmingham as they have been in twentieth-century Jakarta or Sao Paulo. The factories that offered such hope to so many were soon termed "satanic mills." The workers endured intolerable working conditions. Employees were paid far less than they had hoped, as a plentiful supply of workers and rivalry between manufacturers held down wages in the fight to remain cost competitive. Very quickly the towns and cities of Britain became populated with the haves and have-nots. Huge disparities in wealth and living conditions were obvious to all. Slums and abject poverty inhabited the same cities as the great mansions of people with enormous wealth.

Out of this situation grew a new social awareness and sense of obligation and duty. The family unit bound more closely together to ensure survival, and developed a great sense of pride and righteousness as they gradually improved their lot. Charity became a way of life. Rich people gave generously to the poor and established orphanages such as Dr. Barnardo's in London. Local town councils set up workhouses for poor children, although the conditions were rather less than sublime and much derided by Charles Dickens in his novel *Oliver Twist*. In this same novel, Dickens challenges every reader to be charitable and kind to those less fortunate, which is a theme of much of his work and very much in tune with the times in which he lived.

New laws were passed to govern working hours, minimum working age and working conditions. Electoral boundaries were redrawn and processes changed to allow elections in which voter opinions could be more fairly registered. The first steps were taken toward modern medicine and health care. Churchgoers set up new charitable institutions such as the Salvation Army. Above all, a sense of the equality of mankind was built. All people are God's children regardless of age, income, sex, and race. Thus the abolition of slavery was a moral crusade based on the fundamental belief in what we would now call human rights. This in turn reinforced the values of the Christian church, which became deeply involved in the moral behavior and life of its parishioners.

Britain exercised a global moral leadership, and had the military power to apply it. Unfortunately many Christians felt impelled to bring this same sense of righteousness to the far-flung corners of the Empire, and missionaries spread the "good word" to natives who were "ignorant" of the joy that conversion would bring. The intention was entirely altruistic, but the effect was mutinies, uprisings, assassinations, and murderous consequences that were felt in India, Africa, and many other places around the world. So convinced were Britons that their empire was morally and economically beneficial, that Lord Curzon claimed in 1894 that Britain ruled over "the greatest Empire for good that the world has seen."

Out of this sense of altruism and the belief that actions were being taken for the greater good, grew major trends for the twentieth century based on equality, fairness, and charity. Working-class representation and a broader-based democracy soon became compelling issues.

The *Manifesto of the Communist Party*, written by Karl Marx with Friedrich Engels, was published in London in 1848. The results were felt early in the next century. Communism continues to exist today, but in a rather different form than Marx would have anticipated. The independent Labor Party was formed in the late 1800s and soon came to govern Britain. The development of "left wing" versus "right wing" politics quickly destroyed any party that remained standing in the middle, such as Britain's Liberal Party.

The concept of the welfare state was first mooted, and came into being, in the twentieth century. A form of welfare state now exists in virtually every developed country in the world to ensure that no citizen starves. Food stamps, unemployment pay, pensions, and many other social benefits are now mandatory in most first world nations. But the impetus arose from the morals, attitudes and values of the nineteenth century.

The nineteenth century could be summed up as being a time of social and political reform brought about by a new humanitarianism and consciousness of human rights.

Twentieth-Century Values

Cynicism, selfishness, and hedonism were the attitudes and values that underpinned the twentieth century. How did this happen? Although humanitarianism, human rights, and political and social reform had all become established and well entrenched, the twentieth century saw global conflicts of a size and scope never seen before, and some massive social upheavals. Perhaps as a result of the suffering endured in two world wars, people became much more cynical and selfish.

Between the wars, the traditional sense of duty and "doing the right thing" was mocked and derided. The "white man's burden" became a thing to be scoffed at. Britain, for example, became more inward looking and the Empire was seen as a largely unwanted legacy of the previous century. Mahatma Gandhi, the leader of Indian independence, was cheered in the streets during a visit to Britain by a populace who saw him as a champion of the working man, rather than the main irritant to the British colonial government.

The conversion of Britain into a postindustrial society with increasing emphasis on services rather than manufacturing contributed to a rapidly changing foreign policy. Britain no longer needed to protect mineral resources so aggressively. It didn't need to protect trade routes with all those naval and refueling bases such as Malta, Aden, Colombo, Singapore, and Hong Kong. It didn't need all those closed colonial markets to absorb its manufactured goods.

The twentieth-century postindustrial society was much wealthier, and with the underpinning of the welfare state everyone had a financial safety net and disposable income to purchase consumer goods. With this sense of security, people's values became much more selfish and hedonistic. The old virtues of duty, moderation, and pride in your community eroded in the face of fashion, flashiness, and a right to self-expression. Churchgoing declined enormously. From the vast majority of the British population going to church on a Sunday in 1900, less than 10 percent did so by the end of the century. And many of these were immigrants and Catholics rather than Church of England.

The number of new households soared. Affluence and easy credit allowed the purchase of homes, and a desire to "do their own thing" motivated children to leave home as soon as possible. An emphasis on self, personal experience, and individual expression replaced the old values of social commitment, community, and religious values. Duty and empire were replaced by hedonism and commonwealth. This legacy of the twentieth century is still with us. Affluence and credit facilities generate new freedoms, individuality, and the ability to pursue personal lifestyle agendas.

The family unit has become frayed as a commitment to one's self is seen as more important than commitment to parents and other generations. We see this clearly in Asia, where there is a correlation between the economic development of a country and its attitudes to family welfare. Confucianism and commitment to one's parents and family are lowest in Singapore, which has one of the highest per-capita incomes in Asia, whereas "filial piety" and close-knit families are still a central feature of rural China, with its low household income. The same correlation occurs between the affluence of a country and its divorce rate. There has been a steady decline in marriage as an institution, and increase in single family homes in most affluent countries that provide generous government social support systems. Teenage pregnancy is a huge issue, along with crime, drugs, and alcoholism, in many European countries.

The traditional image of Britain as being polite, reserved, and with impeccable manners is now very far from the truth among much of the general population. Despite all this, or perhaps because of it, there is a powerful sense of self-righteousness and personal self-worth that drives attitudes and opinions in Britain and most other Western markets.

The US has driven global aspirations for most of the past 100 years. Hollywood movies and television shows have been a global advertising campaign for the "land of the free": a place where you can say what you want, do what you want, and get whatever you want; where bad guys get shot and the good guys win through. The American ideal drove consumerism, individualism, righteousness, and self-worth.

Are these values and attitudes going to remain with us in the twenty-first century?

The Rise of Communal Spirit

The evidence is that a new communal spirit and value system are rapidly emerging globally. The internet and its social networking sites epitomized by Facebook are already enjoying and growing this new community spirit. Common concerns such as environmentalism have become a powerful connector among people of all ages and nationalities. There is also clear evidence of a return to "traditional values," partly as a result of the economic crisis, and partly in the search for "the meaning of life" by an aging baby boom generation. US President Obama is clearly part of this movement toward a greater community vision and broader values when he says, "Thinking only about yourself, fulfilling your immediate wants and needs, betrays a poverty of ambition."

The election of President Obama also reconfirms the emergence of a more centrist political environment, which is mirrored in many other democracies that have elected "center-left" governments, including

India, Germany, Australia, and Spain. In Britain, the supposedly right-wing Conservative Party could now be mistaken for Tony Blair's New Labor! With the Conservatives having taken the middle ground in the UK, Gordon Brown and his New Labor have to rethink where they stand. They know that moving too left wing would send them back into the political wilderness, so they have to fight again for the hearts and minds of middle-class voters. Britain's Foreign Minister, David Miliband says:

> The economic crisis has unleashed competing forces, both progressive and reactionary. In today's interdependent world, imbalances create insecurity and make us all poorer. Now is our chance to find a new equilibrium.

He sounds a little like a true "son of Tony," and in fact probably represents the attitudinal and political perspective that is likely to drive this new century. Miliband continues, " . . . the wrong response is clear: to pander to protectionism, defer action on climate change, turn inward and succumb to protectionism." He sees "a major opportunity to step up investment in low-carbon energy, transportation, and housing."

These are some of the major areas of change that we will see in the twenty-first century. Politicians will gain and retain power by offering community-oriented policies with stronger government intervention to manage economies and provide citizens with the services they demand. Political parties that follow this centrist political doctrine will retain control of government. Any shifts too far right or left will be quickly rejected in the Age of Selfish Altruism.

Politics is just one area that is being affected by changing values and attitudes. These new values will affect the way we live, how we act, and even how businesses operate. New values and ethics were already emerging ahead of the "great recession," but the recent economic stress has accelerated the changes that are already in progress. Several major trends will power the change in peoples' values, attitudes, and behavior in the twenty-first century. Environmentalism, plus new consumer behavior, and a move toward greater communal consciousness and decision making, are all key factors in this change of values. Adding further impetus is the aging of the global population, and some really scary scientific advancements.

We'll now take a look at the four big trends that are the most powerful forces for change in this century.

Big Trend #1: Save the Planet

. . . it is not about what country you're from, but instead, what planet you're from.

—Earth Hour website

Environmentalism is the new religion. It is advocated by increasingly fervent apostles globally, and followed by an army of committed adherents. It has become a source of deeply held convictions and powerful lifestyle ethics. Environmentalism has become a moral crusade to save the planet we live on, not just for ourselves, but future generations.

The environmental movement has reached the stage where disagreement or dissent is simply not tolerated. Everyone must play their part, or be castigated. Criticism or humor at the expense of the environment is becoming socially unacceptable in the same way as insulting someone's race or religion. The morals and ethics of the environmental movement will affect how we live and what we consume. It will have the same lifestyle strictures as any religion, and will demand strict adherence or penance. Environmentalism will definitely change how we consume.

"Green" beliefs and attitudinal trends have been growing for many years as evidence of environmental and ecological damage became clearer and clearer. The green movement began as a somewhat "hippie" movement, with its leaders looking and sounding as if they were well outside normal consumer lifestyles of the twentieth century. The stunts and provocative actions of Greenpeace increased awareness of the breadth of environmental issues, but were still far from mainstream life. As evidence of environmental damage and the potentially fatal consequences of continuing on the same path have piled up, the need for change has now become firmly embedded in the minds of most people in developed societies. No longer is environmentalism simply a case of saving rainforests from destruction or tigers from extinction. Now it has really come home, and an understanding of the global danger is apparent to everyone from Brazilians to Bangladeshis, and Eskimos and Zulus.

"Greenness" covers many areas, some personal and others altruistic, but the common thread is that we have severely damaged our planet, and we need to stop doing so immediately. If we fail to act quickly, there will be possibly irreversible damage done which may even make future human habitation extremely difficult. The problem with any environmental movement is that clear evidence of the damage usually has to occur before any action is taken. When all are agreed that action is necessary, it is usually in response to almost intolerable conditions that already exist. Action to prevent further damage, or rectify existing problems, tends to happen only when the problem is clearly apparent to everyone.

Problems of the Past

Britain's Midlands area became known as "The Black Country" because of pollution from factories spawned by the Industrial Revolution. Buildings, trees, and the countryside were covered with soot and grime. Darwinians even reported that a species of butterfly gradually evolved its color from light to dark to camouflage itself better on blackened leaves. It took more than a century before any action was taken. London's "fog" was in fact a lethal smog caused by the concentration of coal-burning chimneys in residents' homes as well as emissions from power stations and factories within the city. But nothing was done until the environmental damage caused significant death and considerable disruption.

Perhaps the best example of environmental problems forcing action on a reluctant government occurred in London in 1858. It became known as the Great Stink. The source was the river Thames, which had become the main conduit for all the effluence of London. Every toilet, drain, and gutter ultimately poured its contents into the Thames. The river became a giant sewer, and the fetid water was not only causing extensive environmental damage, it was giving off a truly disgusting aroma. The stench from the polluted Thames was so intense that the Houses of Parliament could not be used. MPs tried closing the windows and covering their mouths and noses with perfumed kerchiefs, but this soon became ineffective. The government was finally forced to act, if only for its own self preservation.

After years of discussion, debate and lobbying, a massive new drainage system was finally constructed to channel waste into sewage farms and then far out to sea. This allowed the Thames to slowly recover and reach the stage of being merely polluted rather than a total sewage stream. London's Embankment, alongside the river, is a highway over the huge Victorian sewage drains underneath. Today the Thames actually has fish in it.

Almost 100 years later, the Great Smog of 1952 finally caused so much death and traffic chaos, that Britain's Clean Air Act was passed four years later in 1956. This mandated smokeless fuel and the relocation of power stations away from city centers. It put an end to London's infamous "fogs," which had become such a famous feature of the city, and I'm sure that the nightingales in Berkeley Square were a lot happier!

As the leading automotive country in the world, America took the lead in reducing exhaust emissions, but only after smog became a massive health issue in many cities, especially Los Angeles. Various clean air acts, lead-free fuel, catalytic converters, and more efficient engines were all mandated by state and federal governments. All these actions only happened because the evidence of health problems and environmental damage was overwhelmingly obvious and completely indisputable. After the measures were taken, the results were equally obvious to see. All the damage was reversible, peoples' lives were saved, and the environment was clearly improved.

On a personal level, I experienced some of this frustration while living in Hong Kong. I'm a keen sailor, and took part in the yacht club races on the harbor every weekend. It was soon obvious to me that the harbor was becoming very polluted. The cross-harbor swim had been canceled the year I arrived in Hong Kong because the water quality was becoming a concern. I noticed that the amount of plastic, Styrofoam, and even dead animals floating in the water was increasing significantly as each year passed. Also, when the sun went down in the evening, one could see that the level of smog was getting more intense. The particles in the air created wonderful sunsets, but were clearly a cause for concern.

However, air and water pollution was so far down the awareness and interest level of companies in Hong Kong that people laughed at me for mentioning it in the late 1980s. "It is the price of progress" was the refrain I heard in Hong Kong, as well as China, Taiwan, Korea, Malaysia, and many other markets to which I traveled. Environmental issues were very much Western problems and had no role in the rapid development of Asian economies. Pollution was simply a cost of business. And if Western countries caused so much pollution when they grew, why shouldn't Asia have the same opportunity? No discrimination please!

Chinese Pollution

Today China is the number one producer of carbon dioxide in the world, and air pollution is a key inhibitor to business in Hong Kong. The quality of air is so bad in Hong Kong and many of the cities in China that many expatriate businessmen refuse to move there to avoid exposing their families to the damage it can cause. Water pollution is a huge issue all across China after several disgraceful industrial spills and emissions, some of which required the Government to supply bottled water to entire towns and cities. Food and health standards have had to be dramatically improved after a series of contamination scandals, including the Sanlu milk powder disaster. Environmental issues have now leapt to the forefront of political and corporate life in China, and draconian punishments are now being meted out to offenders.

The greens may long have been a political force in a developed country such as Germany, but developing countries around the world are now rapidly adopting the same policies and outlook as they see the same problems. Unfortunately, the damage being done to the entire planet is only now becoming accepted as fact, after decades of dire warnings and anecdotal evidence. The big issue is that if we don't act quickly, the damage may *not* be reversible. The ozone layer may not rebuild itself. The polar icecaps may not simply reappear. The climate may not simply settle down again. Then we're all in deep trouble.

The Need to Act

Global warming has been likened to boiling a frog in water, although I prefer to think of a crab or lobster as a slightly more attractive analogy. The imperceptible increase in temperature is probably quite pleasant at first, a little like emerging from the Ice Age. Then it gets a lot warmer, and, although quite noticeable, is not unpleasant. Only when it starts to get really hot do we feel any discomfort, and then at boiling point it's all too late to think about anything other than survival. The Earth hasn't reached boiling point yet, but a lot of people are noticing that we are moving up in temperature from warm to a lot warmer. There is clear evidence that rising average temperatures are the cause of icecaps melting, water levels rising, and weather patterns changing. The issue is no longer one of keeping the temperature from rising, we need to turn the heat down immediately.

Most of us imagine that it is like turning down a gas flame under the pot of water. But we should think of what we're doing as boiling water on an electric stove, not a gas range. The element doesn't just turn down like a gas flame, it takes time to reduce its convection heat, and while it does so, the pot of water keeps getting hotter.

So even if we turned down carbon emissions today, we have already set in motion sufficient heat that the Earth will continue to get hotter for many years yet to come. This is the reason that so much emphasis is suddenly being placed on finding alternative energy sources and reducing carbon emissions. We need to take drastic action, and we must do so immediately before the pot actually boils.

Retailer Marks & Spencer in the UK has launched an environmental program to achieve carbon neutrality by 2012 by "working with our customers and our suppliers to combat climate change, reduce waste, safeguard natural resources, trade ethically and build a healthier nation." It calls this program Plan A. Why is it called Plan A? Because according to its vision, there is no Plan B. I think this is what every government is now coming to understand. There is no Plan B.

Food

The leading edge of environmental concern was perhaps in foodstuffs. The use of DDT and other pesticides killed insects, birds, and animals, and was getting into the human food chain. Again, action was taken only after the damaging evidence was clearly apparent, but the DDT ban was probably the first really global action taken to protect the environment that I am aware of. New less harmful pesticides were introduced, but concern about *any* chemical or preservative damaging plant, animal, and human life eventually led to the demand for organic food, free of pesticides and harmful chemicals.

The importance of clean earth and water, and the danger of chemicals entering the food chain, was graphically illustrated in the Japanese city of Minamata, which had a disease named after it. Minamata disease is caused by mercury poisoning, and results in severe neurological problems that lead to a range of physical defects. The disease can also be congenital, affecting fetuses while still in the womb, and severely damages the resulting child. In many cases, Minamata disease leads to death after considerable suffering. It was first discovered in 1956, and was subsequently found to be caused by wastewater containing high levels of mercury released by Chisso Corporation's chemical factory into the local bay. The mercury spread into the surrounding waters and was absorbed by fish and shellfish. This highly toxic seafood was consumed by the local community and caused mercury poisoning. The full story of the Minamata disaster is quite extraordinary, and contributed to the stereotype of a cruel and uncaring corporation only concerned with profit that knowingly damaged the local population and covered up its action for decades.

Chisso Corporation began contaminating the waters in Minamata Bay in 1932, and through lies, deceit, and concerted pressure on local and national government, was allowed to continue to do so until 1968. The factory had long engaged in disputes with local fishermen, and had paid compensation twice in prewar years, and again in 1959 after fishing catches had declined by a staggering 91 percent between 1953 and 1957. Local residents had noticed cats acting as though they were mad, and birds dying after eating seaweed, but the first cases of human mercury poisoning emerged in 1956. After two years of investigation the cause was confirmed as mercury, and the Chisso chemical factory as the culprit.

So the company moved its wastewater outlet from Minamata Bay to the nearby river to "solve the problem." This action caused mercury to travel out to the open sea and up the coast, creating a new wave of human damage. Then the company claimed to have set up a filtration plant to clean the water. This was bogus machinery, and the company had simply moved the mercury outlet again. Any compensation paid to those local people with Minamata disease was pitifully small as government arbitrators sided with the company and the employment it provided. Only when a different city elsewhere in Japan suffered the same disease and successfully prosecuted the local chemical company did others around Japan come to the aid of the people of Minamata.

There was a citizen's movement that gradually gained national support, and media coverage exerted greater and greater pressure on the company and the government. The Japanese government finally issued an official conclusion that mercury was the cause of Minamata disease 12 years after it was first reported, and four months after Chisso stopped the process that was the cause of mercury use.

A court case ensued and the findings created global coverage of corporate cover-up, government collusion, and the galvanizing effect of "people power." This "citizens' uprising" is said by many to mark the first demonstration of true democracy ever seen in Japan, and the issue was environmentalism. Lawsuits and compensation payments continue as the damage lingers on right up to the present.

In the US, the dangers of toxic waste came to the fore with the Love Canal scandal. The Hooker Chemical and Plastics Corporation buried 21,000 tons of toxic waste in an area that was subsequently built upon to create a school and a housing suburb. Residents complained of noxious odors, dying trees and plants, odd residues, and significant medical problems. Although the problem was quickly identified, admission of liability and subsequent action were slow to occur, and only a national media frenzy drove the government into action. Residents were moved to a new location, compensated for their homes, and Hooker was found guilty of negligence and fined $129 million. Love Canal again cast the chemical company as callous and uncaring because it fought every attempt to find it culpable for the human damage. These were the days before corporate social responsibility (CSR) programs had become an integral part of corporate life. The scandal stimulated the creation of new legislation in the US that holds polluters responsible for their actions.

Is it any wonder then consumers demanded foodstuffs completely free of pesticides and chemicals? This is the reason that organic foods were slowly introduced to the market. They now have a solid share of the grocery market, but certainly a lot less than was expected many years ago. This is probably thanks to greater confidence in the agricultural system as a result of tighter legislation, and concerted efforts by corporations to portray themselves as trustworthy corporate citizens.

In addition, consumers can't help but choose produce that *looks* perfect, and often organic foods appear more gnarled and scarred in their "natural state." Research and subsequent consumer purchase patterns indicate that consumers will pay 5–15 percent more for organic foods than for comparable products that have been exposed to chemicals or preservatives. However, what they say and what they actually do when faced with a higher price can be rather different.

Finally, a general confidence in health standards and a belief that organic is "nice to have, rather than need to have" mean that the eating habits of the general population have not significantly shifted toward organic food. And debates about exactly what constitutes "organic" have sown some additional confusion. Organic foods have never gained the broad-scale market share that was expected by many companies, and have almost been overshadowed by other related causes such as the "fair trade" emphasis that has become so prominent recently.

Food Self-Sufficiency

One of Michelle Obama's first acts when she and her husband took residence in the White House was to announce that she would be planting a 1,100 square foot organic vegetable garden. It will grow a variety of green vegetables and herbs, and it will be accompanied by a beehive, so that the White House will have its own natural honey. This is likely to be an increasing trend among households in the US and elsewhere as compulsory composting of foodstuffs and continued awareness of the ease (and enjoyment) with which vegetables and fruit can be grown drive people into a broader use of their backyards as vegetable and herb gardens.

In the UK, the National Trust is masterminding a plan to get Britain's biggest landowners to turn over some of their land to families, who would grow their own fruit and vegetables. The intention of the "grow your own" campaign is to reduce carbon emissions from food imports and to create healthier eating habits.

"There is a tangible desire for people to reconnect with the soil," said the director general of the National Trust. "Townies" and "newbie" growers will get support from the 390,000 members of the Royal Horticultural Society, and the Garden Organic charity.

Food self-sufficiency is not just a personal theme for this century, but a national one as well. The recent economic crisis has revealed that every country knows that protectionist measures damage everyone, but it also showed that the importance of self-sufficiency in every area possible would safeguard a country against pricing and supply vagaries in the future. The massive spikes in food costs in 2007 and 2008 have contributed to many new national policies demanding food self-sufficiency.

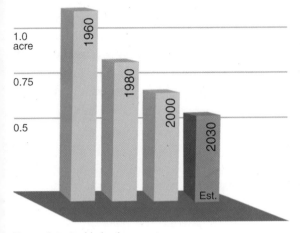

Figure 5.1 Arable land per capita

Governments all over the world have decided that their countries should become as self-sufficient as possible.

I was in Malaysia recently, and was surprised to hear that the government had decided to become self-sufficient in rice by 2020. This is a low-margin crop, and Malaysia's arable land could be used to grow much more value-added crops than rice. But apparently the recent shock of being unable to obtain sufficient rice at a reasonable price from neighboring countries was so traumatic that the government immediately changed its agricultural policy.

Food supply shortages are most likely to be an increasing feature of the twenty-first century. The reasons are pretty straightforward.

- The global population will grow by 50 percent over the next 50 years.

   The UN estimates that there was 1.1 acres of arable farmland per person in 1960. This had almost halved by 2000, and will decline again to about half an acre or less per person by 2030 (see figure 5.1). That is not a lot of land to grow enough food for every person on the planet.

   Food consumption has exceeded production for several years, and stockpiles built up in the past have been reduced or eliminated. "Carryover stocks" of foodstuffs are now at some of the lowest levels seen for a long time.

- Increasing affluence is creating demand for more food, and more expensive food.

   Dietary habits in China and other developing countries are changing significantly with a much greater demand for meats and dairy foods. The huge increase in cattle to meet this demand requires a lot more feed. The USDA estimates that it requires seven pounds of grain to produce one pound of meat. So cows are now competing with humans for corn and soy beans, and with farmers for the right to graze rather than the ability to plant crops.

- Biofuels are creating increased demand for foodstuffs.
  If the increase in population and greater demand for food weren't enough of a problem, the commitment to nonpolluting biofuels has increased competition for available crops and driven up prices. The result is that demand for basic foodstuffs and "low price" stable foods is rising significantly in a world with less and less land per capita to produce it. So the poorest people, who already spend half to three-quarters of their income on food, will suffer as the price of corn, soy, and other staples inexorably increases.

- Land is being dedicated to higher-priced crops.
  In tropical parts of Asia, particularly Indonesia, land is being used for added-value crops such as palm oil and rubber, rather than for rice or low-cost staples. The demand for new palm oil land has resulted in the wholesale destruction of forests in Borneo and other parts of Southeast Asia. This is creating air pollution due to slash and burn farming techniques (the infamous "haze" that is affecting Singapore as well as many other parts of the region as I write) and enormous ecological damage. Wildlife sanctuaries are being damaged, and there seems to be absolutely no interest or concern from the Indonesian government. Brazil doesn't seem to be a lot better. We read every day about rainforests being illegally logged, or burned to clear land for agriculture. Brazil is now the soybean capital of the world, but at what cost to its natural assets and ecosystem?

George Soros, Jim Rogers, and many other high-profile investors have a new investment focus on land and related farming facilities. So does BlackRock Investments and many pension funds. The reason is that "limited land and water resources will automatically lead to increased valuations of productive land," according to the director general of the International Food Policy Research Institute. He also mentions that land use goes hand in hand with water consumption, and that water scarcity may become an even bigger issue than land.

Climate Change

Climate change is creating global disruption to agriculture. Not only are there problems with drought or floods, but the climate of entire growing regions is changing. This means that they have to change to growing different crops with different techniques. Rising sea levels may cause additional issues because low-lying arable land may become saline or simply disappear under the encroaching sea.

Competition for arable land will increase prices. China has 20 percent of the world's population, but only 7 percent of the arable land. So it is investing $5 billion in Africa in a series of agricultural programs to ensure food sources for its people. Many Middle Eastern countries have virtually no arable land, so Qatar, Saudi Arabia, and Abu Dhabi are making significant acquisitions of great swathes of Africa and Asia. I'm sure that this is driven by investment opportunity as much as the need for a secure food supply, but nevertheless it all adds pressure to land prices.

In late 2008, Daewoo from South Korea announced a deal to lease a staggering half of all arable land in Madagascar! The local outrage quite rightly contributed to a *coup d'état*.

The gains from the Green Revolution are over, and it may now actually be causing damage. The British scholar Thomas Malthus developed various theories about population growth, and in his *An Essay on the Principle of Population* said, "The power of population is indefinitely greater than the power in the earth to produce subsistence for man." Malthus observed that population growth was exponential, whereas agricultural expansion was linear. So Malthus calculated that agricultural expansion couldn't match the rate of growth of the population. He concluded that war, famine, and disease, plus delayed marriage and birth control would provide limits to human population growth. So humans would have only enough to eat if these "Malthusian" effects were felt.

Although he is logically correct, he based his logic on the assumption that the amount of land available for agriculture does not increase dramatically, and that improved agricultural output per acre does not increase significantly. However, the amount of land being converted to agriculture keeps on increasing, and a Green Revolution over the past 50 years has massively increased crop yields. So although population has increased hugely since Malthus' time, food production has been able to keep pace with the growing need.

The Green Revolution delivered more intensive agriculture using higher yielding crops, but it depended on plentiful water supply, fertilizers, and insecticides. However, the big gains from this revolution are over and yields are now flat in those places that adopted the techniques decades ago. In addition, in many areas the extensive use of water has lowered the water table, and intensive use of manufactured fertilizers and insecticides has stripped nutrients from the soil. There is also clear evidence that chemicals have entered the food chain in farming communities.

The solution is genetics, because the code of most plants is now known and can be modified. Genetically modified food could increase yields by creating drought-resistant strains, reduced-fertilizer grains, and many other types of "bespoke" varieties. However, there is deep distrust of genetically modified food, or "Frankenstein food" as it called in some tabloid newspapers.

Essentially the argument is no different from that of the DDT debate all those years ago. If we start eating genetically modified food, what will it do to us when we eat it? And to the birds and animals that eat it? Will it cause genetic problems in humans that could be damaging or fatal? The short-term solution seems to be better crop rotation with diversified crops, natural fertilizers, and greater husbandry of resources. The long-term answer is population stability, not agricultural output expansion.

So the next 50 years are likely to see various food shortages and continuously increasing food prices, with the occasional surplus "busts" such as with overproduction of soybeans when biofuels are discarded in favor of other fuel/power sources. Finding a balance between producing enough food to feed an increasing population, and preventing continued ecological damage, such as destruction of the tropical rainforests, is going to require a mixture of diplomacy and legislation, and far greater commitment from the governments involved.

Standing in stark contrast to the issues we face with food production and increasing prices, the biggest health issue in most developed countries is overeating. During the past 50 years, we have seen some serious damage to humans occurring through poor dietary habits. Fast food outlets have offered inexpensive, high-calorie food to the masses, and mass is what we now have. Obesity is endemic in many Western countries, notably the US, Australia, and the UK, where as much as 40 percent of the population could be classified as obese. Even in China and other Asian nations, a new level of child obesity is creating great concern. Latest data show that 20 percent of US four-year-olds are obese, and we are seeing similar trends in Asian countries as their affluence increases and diet changes.

Although it seems laughable, apparently obesity does contribute to global warming. The London School of Hygiene and Medicine claims that the UK uses 19 percent more food energy than 40 years previously. "When it comes to food consumption, moving about in a heavy body is like driving around in a gas guzzler," and food production is a major source of greenhouse gases, said the study. It also indicated that on average, each fat person is responsible for a ton of carbon dioxide emissions a year more than a thin person. So a billion obese people worldwide would generate a billion extra tons of carbon dioxide. Lose weight and save the planet! Despite these trends toward obesity, there is now a much greater awareness of the need for healthy eating. Food manufacturers are being encouraged to reduce salt, sugar, and damaging fats in their products. Fast-food outlets are being forced to change their menus to incorporate healthier, less fattening foods. Food labeling clearly indicating calories is now being legislated. Schools are putting greater emphasis on teaching the importance of fruit and vegetable consumption as well as the importance of major food groups. In addition, additives that may cause behavioral abnormalities, particularly among children, are being eliminated from foods and drinks. Supermarkets are now beginning to ban products that contain certain additives that may cause hyperactivity or even brain damage.

Packaging and Recycling

To achieve true sustainability, we must reduce our "garbage index" — that which we permanently throw away into the environment that will not be naturally recycled for reuse—to near zero. Productive activities must be organized as closed systems. Minerals and other non-biodegradable resources, once taken from the ground, must become a part of society's permanent capital stock and be recycled in perpetuity. Organic materials may be disposed into the natural ecosystems, but only in ways that assure that they are absorbed back into the natural production system.
—David Korten, author

The Consumer Century created more waste than had ever been imagined in previous times. The advent of plastics, cellophane, and other non-biodegradable materials allowed manufactures to provide cheaper, more elaborate packaging to increase the appeal of their products and entice consumers. By the end of the past century, the packaging and branding were as important as the product itself. This is at its zenith in Japan, where gift packaging is extremely elaborate, beautiful, and expensive. I was often amazed that some of the most stunning packaging I saw in Tokyo during gift-giving seasons contained only bars of soap, or cigarettes, or a few rice biscuits. The cost and value of the packaging were many times greater than the cost of the contents.

Fortunately, most people's thoughts are now turning toward the need for recycled and biodegradable packaging. This does include Japan, where *furoshiki* are making a comeback as wrappings for gifts. *Furoshiki* are traditional, colorful, patterned cotton cloths that can be used as wrapping, and then reused as a hand towel or for other purposes in the home. An added cultural benefit is that Japanese now have to relearn folding and wrapping techniques using *furoshiki* to beautify their packaging.

Companies all over the world are re-evaluating their packaging to reduce its bulk and waste, and ensure that it is environmentally friendly. This stretches from household goods and food manufacturers using simpler packaging all the way up to Veuve Clicquot champagne. The bubbly claims that its new eco-friendly gift box "requires no plastic; is made from paper from trees under the management of the Forest Stewardship Council; contains less than 5 percent inks, solvents and glues; is recyclable; and can be optimized for transportation, thus reducing CO_2 emissions."

Veuve Clicquot is ahead of the game and anticipating the demands and new values of its consumer: I want to celebrate and get really silly, but I don't want to cause any environmental problems when I enjoy myself.

There is a huge global movement developing over bottled water, which many claim causes unnecessary use of plastics and fuel for transport. One slide show I viewed recently indicates that more than 28 billion plastic water bottles are produced each year, of which 86 percent end up in the garbage. The production of the bottles contributes 25 million tons of greenhouse gases, and spending on bottled water amounts to $100 billion. It is also claimed that harmful chemicals leach from the bottles into the water over time. The conclusion is that bottled water contributes to major environmental hazards and diverts funds that could be better spent elsewhere.

"Precycling" is a new word that was coined to describe the need for thoughtfulness at the point of purchase, not just the point of throwing out. Precycling encourages people to reduce consumption, reuse items, and to think about the environmental impact before purchase. In the future, precycling and recycling will be part of the same equation and equally important in their affect on consumer purchasing patterns.

Many claims made by environmentalists can sometimes be viewed as exaggerated or more than a little suspect, but they are given credence because their motive is usually entirely altruistic, with the best interests of all of us at heart. However, if any manufacturer makes environmental claims that later prove to be false, it will feel the wrath of both the consumer and the government. Businesses are built on trust, and a breach of that trust can be very damaging to their reputation and finances. Government will increasingly be both referee and coach. The British environment secretary for example, has proposed fines of up to £50,000 on companies that fail to cut back on plastic and cardboard. He is suggesting that supermarkets be required to provide refill services, to encourage the reuse of containers of coffee, detergent, and other "staples." And recyclable materials such as glass and aluminum may be banned from landfill sites.

The ubiquitous plastic shopping bag that now litters the world is being banned in country after country, or there is a charge for its use. When I asked for a plastic bag in an Australian supermarket recently, my request was received as though I'd admitted to having a very nasty disease. Yes, I felt duly shamed by the shop assistant and the tutting and sniffing of those people behind me in the queue: "He didn't bring his own bag! How irresponsible." Some supermarkets in the UK now have a recycling bin at the point of checkout, where consumers can dump unwanted packaging on the products they have purchased.

Recycling is now mandatory in the EU and many other countries. Recycling quotas are mandated for every local council in the UK, for example, and consumers fined for putting the wrong items in the various collection bins. Garbage collections are being reduced, and consumers induced to create or buy compost bins to dispose of food and organic waste. Maximum weights of garbage are also being imposed and additional local taxes charged to those exceeding their household weight limit. All these new government measures are designed to reduce garbage mountains and incineration requirements. They are an imposition on the general population, but it is a responsibility that citizens are now prepared to accept for the good of the planet.

Global Warming

In the past, it was possible to destroy a village, a town, a region, even a country. Now it is the whole planet that has come under threat. This fact should compel everyone to face a basic moral consideration; from now on, it is only through a conscious choice and then deliberate policy that humanity will survive.
—Pope John Paul II

There is massive international support for measures to prevent further global warming. The Kyoto Agreement set objectives for individual countries to reduce their "carbon footprint," that is the weight of carbon emissions they produce per year. Unfortunately, the world's biggest current and future polluters, the US, China, and India, have not "signed up" to any specific objectives. However, consumer pressure, increasing environmental problems, and the overwhelming evidence of climate change are now forcing these governments to act. There are now clear signs that China and the US at least will agree to action that may well be a benchmark for all other countries, both developed and developing.

The issue facing all counties is *how* to reduce their "carbon footprint" without adversely affecting economic growth and the standard of living of their citizens. Offsetting one's carbon footprint has generated a multibillion carbon-trading industry as companies and countries try to offset their excess carbon by selling it to others. This may be a clever method of achieving short-term goals, but it isn't a long-term solution.

The root of the problem is our reliance on coal and oil power. It is critical to almost every economy because it generates our electricity and powers our vehicles. No nation can hope either to advance economically or to sustain its standard of living without electrical power. Most of this electrical power is generated by carboniferous fossil fuels that give off carbon dioxide as they burn, and these emissions are causing damage to the upper atmosphere and the air we breathe.

The earth maintained a volume of about 280 parts per million of carbon dioxide in the air for the 10,000 or so years up to the Industrial Revolution. Then the number steadily began to rise as we burned wood, coal, and oil. Today we have about 384 parts of carbon dioxide in our air, and this is rising very fast with the rapid industrialization of China, India, and other developing nations. This is not to mention the continued burning of rainforests, primitive slash and burn crop rotation, and even the flatulence of an increasing number of cows and sheep as we eat more meat. Scientists calculate that a carbon dioxide level of 450 parts per million will be catastrophic, and we will easily achieve that this century if current trends continue.

Climate change is already affecting weather patterns, and the El Niño effect in the Pacific, the great drought in Australia, super hurricanes like Katrina, and changing monsoon patterns in Asia are all evidence of the change that is occurring.

There is also a clear understanding that mineral resources are becoming scarcer, and the environmental damage caused by the more aggressive search for new mineral sources is unsustainable. More "responsible" attitudes are now washing over into almost every area of life, while we search for sustainable solutions for the future. A recent BBC poll said that 87 percent of travelers would prefer, and pay extra, for methods of travel, accommodation, and holidays that they felt were less damaging to the environment. The same poll found that 29 percent of British consumers will not travel to Antarctica or the Galapagos because they are concerned that their footprint would damage a fragile environment.

There are very few companies that do not have a CSR policy, and most public companies now produce an annual CSR report, which puts additional pressure on the business to continue to improve its environmental safety standards and "clean" operations.

Efforts to find alternative energy sources are now intensifying, driven by political, consumer and economic pressure. A wide number of noncarbon, sustainable energy alternatives are being explored, many becoming much more viable as technological advances provide the conversion techniques to make them much more productive. These intensified efforts to find sustainable power are not just due to the environmental problems of using fossil fuels, they are also driven by uncertainty of supply and unstable costs. The first oil shock in 1973 created an acute awareness of the vulnerability that countries and companies faced when having to import all their domestic fuel needs. Subsequent surges in price have heightened that awareness, as has many countries having to import fuel from others that they do not entirely trust.

The bulk of the world's oil supplies emanate from the Middle East, which is a hot bed of Islamic fundamentalism that is appalled at the lifestyle and morals of the "West." Russia is the principal supplier to much of Europe, so any policy differences raise the question of supplies drying up. Ukraine has felt the annoyance of Russia on a couple of occasions already as punishment for its pro-European shift. The result has been price increases and subsequent cessation of supplies. The only thing that has saved Ukraine from freezing to death has been that gas pipelines pass through it en route to Europe. So stopping supplies to Ukraine also affects countries in Europe. It is little wonder then that various European countries are looking for alternative energy sources. The French, and to a lesser extent Britain turned to nuclear energy. But the potential for devastating environmental damage will always mitigate the use of nuclear fuel.

In his book, *Hot, Flat, and Crowded*, Thomas Friedman mentions a famous Chinese saying, "When the wind changes direction, there are those who build walls and those who build windmills." The Danes took this advice to heart. Denmark, being a flat windswept country, decided that windpower offered the best opportunity to provide an alternative energy source. Windmills and wind farms are now found all across the country. Over the past 30 years, Denmark has gradually increased the amount of electricity it generates from windpower to almost 20 percent of its total output. This is twice as much as any other country. It has become a leader in windpower technology, as well as conservation. The country realized that obtaining alternative energy was part of the equation, but using less was equally important. Passing legislation to encourage businesses and homes to use less electricity, and increasing taxes on carbon fuels, combined to reduce power consumption. Today, Denmark has the lowest energy use per point of GDP in the world.

Windpower is much beloved by governments as a short-term replacement for oil- and coal-fired generators, because the technology is already available, and the efforts can be seen in the form of giant windmills that dot the landscape. Windpower will continue to be a factor for the long term, but already there are strong environmental concerns about the destruction of birds in the blades of the windmills and the scarring of beautiful natural landscapes with giant, ugly pillars. So windpower will most likely be increasingly limited to coastal wind farms and locations where their unsightliness will not create an army of Don Quixotes bent on their destruction.

Solar energy is the most appealing alternative energy source, and solar panels are becoming significantly more efficient in converting the sun's rays into usable power. At present, large, ugly solar panels are still fairly inefficient, and a major problem is the storage of power that is created during the day, but more consumed in the evening. However, the advent of thinner, more efficient panels, and panels that are bendable is making "micropower" much more feasible. By building the panels into a building or fixed product such as a sunshade or umbrella, it is now possible to allow every home and building to generate its own electricity. This is one of the big product changes we'll see this century, and we'll talk about the implications later.

Tidal and water power will also be a factor, but for many landlocked or arid parts of the world it will simply not be an option. However, those countries, such as Norway, with a decent coastline, especially with inlets, fjords, and major rivers, will be devoting to considerable energy (if you'll pardon the pun) to tidal and even saltwater power.

Solar, wind, and tidal systems are all becoming much bigger factors in the generation of power, but so are humans. California Fitness in Hong Kong uses the power generated from use of the exercise machines to light the gym facility. London dance clubs are doing the same thing by using the dancefloor to create energy.

Every person in the future will be expected to generate all the power they need himself or herself. If you want power, you will soon have to generate it yourself or face punishingly high charges for centrally delivered power. This may come from wearing mini-generators that create power through movement, much like an automatic watch, or ensuring that your dwelling is completely energy self-sufficient.

Interestingly, in Denmark there is a certain amount of competition among households and individuals to see who can be the most green. Local communities give out trophies for the "greenest village"; corporations reward the "greenest employees"; governments provide certificates of excellence to buildings, cities, and towns. Given human nature, and our desire to be competitive and to have fun, it seems likely that environmentalism as a "sport" is most likely to become widespread. It will all contribute to the same sense of individual responsibility playing a key role in communal action towards sustainability.

Governments are now developing much more aggressive plans, and creating legislation, to achieve sustainability. Singapore recently published a "Green Blueprint," which set up three core areas for dramatic improvement:

- Buildings: 80 percent will need to be eco-friendly and have a "green mark" certificate by 2030. This will involve new building standards, subsidies to retrofit solar panels and other energy saving and energy-efficient devices to old buildings.

- Air quality: achieve a 25 percent reduction in fine air particles and other emissions by 2020 through the expansion of public transport facilities, electric vehicles, hybrid diesel buses, new vehicle filters, and an expanded bike path network. The city already has vehicle congestion charges in its downtown areas and huge taxes on private cars to encourage use of public transportation. In addition, cars can only operate for 10 years, then need to be scrapped, so the newer engines are cleaner and more efficient.

- Park and green area expansion: expansion of existing parkland and creation of new parkland, including rooftop and carpark-top gardens and landscaping ("skyrise greenery"), and new wetland creation.

New York is facing the same problems as Singapore. Both have high-density populations and simply do not wish to keep building more power stations on scarce land. Both are faced with the need to significantly reduce not only power use, but also the dangerous emissions that severe traffic causes. And both want to create an attractive, green environment for its citizens and the tourists that flock to the cities. New York's Mayor Michael Bloomberg unveiled PlaNYC on Earth Day 2007. The PlaNYC program objectives and plans are very similar to Singapore's, with an immediate focus on retrofitting buildings to make them far more energy efficient, hybrid transportation, bike lanes, and new green spaces.

Although admirable, these initiatives will only moderate or temporarily reduce the causes of global warming until technology can help deliver fundamental change. Government will be the legislative force that provides the blueprints and legislative mandates for environmental goals, but genuine sustainability will come from bottom-up individual actions that all combine to reduce the demand for centrally developed electrical power and products using oil.

The most important of these developments will be that every building will have to generate all its own power from sustainable energy. Every house, apartment building, and office building will become a micropower station to generate its own sustainable energy and become self-sufficient. It will have solar panels, rooftop wind tunnels, and batteries to store power. Some dwellings may be able to use underground thermal power for heating, or recycle biomass. Biofuels may also play a part initially, but as with hybrid cars will eventually be replaced by clean energy that requires no combustion at all.

Once the technology is at a stage where it is efficient and completely viable, housing permits will simply not be issued without a sustainability certificate. And old buildings will be given a financial incentive and a limited time frame to make themselves energy self-sufficient. Only when buildings become energy self-sufficient will the demand for power stations and other centrally generated power be significantly diminished. Just as cars making the conversion to electric power is the ultimate solution to reducing carbon emissions from vehicles, so will homes becoming energy self-sufficient reduce emissions from power stations.

Interestingly, the US Army is already taking this idea to heart. It is installing wind turbines and solar-cell systems, and using geothermal power in barracks and other buildings. The intention is to reduce cost, but also to make army units less dependent on traditionally generated power sources that are susceptible to disruption. The idea is to make all troops self-sufficient, so that their electronic equipment remains fully functional under any operational condition. This same philosophy will apply to individual housing. Every home will need to be self-sufficient under any economic or climatic condition. Then it will not have to depend on any national power grid for its energy.

Already many housing authorities in the UK have different grades of environmental approval for new home construction. The most draconian level demands that a house be fully self-sufficient in power. However, given the technical limitations, most homes are being given a mid-grade approval, which insists on solar panels, long-life lights, special insulation, and various other features. In Japan, the most robust part of the otherwise slow housing construction market are the new eco-homes, which provide significant power self-sufficiency.

Electric cars and bikes that are recharged at home will also benefit from homes that generate their own power. Free "fill-ups" will bring joy to many car owners. The benefit to consumers will be considerable: no more electricity or fuel bills. This will dramatically improve household disposable income.

How soon will this happen? It will happen when solar panels, mini-windmills, geothermal heating, and other sustainable technologies create a level of energy conversion sufficient to satisfy all household needs, 24 hours a day, 365 days a year. This will almost certainly require power storage facilities, which means that battery technology will again be needed to power the house as well as the car. Given the rapid strides being taken in solar, wind, and battery technology, I suspect that a fully integrated system sufficient to meet the needs of most homes cannot be more than five years away. So we will likely see home and office building permits being conditional on self-generated energy supply by 2020 or before.

Water

Every house will also become a mini-reservoir and water-recycling plant that will save, filter, and recycle water, so that it may be used many times over. Houses will soon be expected to collect rain water to reduce dependency on "mains water" and prevent the destruction of underground water tables.

I was in Adelaide, Australia, recently, and visited a friend. His house and apparently most others in Adelaide have large storage tanks built into the construction to act as a reservoir for the rainwater that is gathered from the roof of the house. The house uses this water for washing, flushing, and watering. Only drinking water is collected from the mains. The rainwater is filtered and reused several times, and is eventually disposed of as "grey water" to irrigate the garden.

More efficient filtration systems will allow the almost permanent recycling of water. Approximately 10 percent of Singapore's water is recycled sewage passed through a "new water" filtration system. This "new water" filtration process is being refined and expanded, so that it will eventually provide a large proportion of the country's water. It is also being bottled and sold as commercially attractive pure water. Over the years "new water" will complement and reduce the amount of reservoirs needed to hold water, and potentially reduce the amount of imported water from nearby Malaysia. The same principle will apply to homes. They will need to become self-sufficient and only use mains water in the event of emergency or sudden need.

Water is the almost unmentionable bomb in any climate change discussions, but its availability is already becoming a major issue in many countries. I holidayed in Jordan a while ago, and water availability is now a massive survival issue for the country. The Jordan River is now a fetid, tiny stream, barely a few yards wide. So much water has been siphoned off to irrigate crops on both sides of the river that it has been reduced to a tiny version of what it once was. The real insanity is that huge amounts of water are being taken to irrigate watermelon and other water-intensive crops in this extremely arid area.

I visited an oasis town in Jordan that my driver used to live in. He remembered boating and fishing there as a boy just 20 years previously. Big villas stand around the "lake," where the wealthy would have weekend homes in this lovely place. Lawrence of Arabia set up his headquarters in an old fort that had been there for hundreds of years. Clearly this was once a little bit of paradise in a harsh desert. Today there is no water at all. Absolutely none. It was all siphoned off to provide drinking water to the capital city of Amman. The houses lie in disrepair amid the dust blowing across the dried bed of the lake. Water is now being piped to Amman from the underground natural reservoir beneath the sands of Wadi Rhum in the south of Jordan, but no one knows how long that will last, especially as the city's population increases dramatically as a "safe haven" in a troubled region. There is talk of desalinization plants to bring water from the Red Sea, but the cost is enormous for a poor country.

Seeing the water problems in Jordan, and then in Australia shortly afterward, really brings home the need for recycling and conservation. But again, the solution will be to make every house, apartment, and office building as self-sufficient as possible by converting them into mini-reservoirs and recycling plants.

A vision of the future is being created in the emirate of Abu Dhabi, where the first zero-carbon and zero-waste city is being built. Masdar will be almost entirely driven by solar energy, and will use 75 percent less electricity and 60 percent less water than other developments that have a similar resident population of 50,000 and a daily intake of 40,000 commuters. The city is a fabulous project, but it is not entirely revolutionary, because it simply applies the techniques we outlined for all of our homes and lifestyle in the future. Masdar does have some innovations like cooling towers that use negative pressure to draw hot air up and out of the enclosed city, and cooling that more efficiently circulates from the ground up.

It's a great initiative, and should provide a whole range of learning for future building developments. However, these mega-developments will be less important than the broad-scale application of the same principles to individual buildings in every country in the world. Ultimately, to make any significant change, everyone will have to play a part. This sense of individual responsibility within a communal framework will be the central pillar of consumer values in the twenty-first century.

There is clear evidence that governments are now realizing that environmental issues are becoming more critical and that sustainable energy is a key economic opportunity in the twenty-first century. Asian and other developing countries seem to be more acutely aware of the economic benefits and opportunities, perhaps because they have suffered many environmental catastrophes in the rush to grow their GNPs and they lack the domestic supplies of oil and gas their economies demand. Japan, China, and South Korea, for example, are discussing how to share their knowledge and expertise to develop new "green" technologies and develop new commercial opportunities. Korea has "low-carbon green growth" as a new slogan for economic development, and recently devoted 81 percent of its financial stimulus package to green projects. In addition, the country will spend $40 billion to create "a new paradigm of qualitative growth that uses less energy and is more compatible with environmental sustainability."

The US government is putting the economic opportunities of sustainable energy as a key rationale for new environmental programs, and is earmarking $50 billion for alternative energy programs. European countries are all scrambling to encourage the growth of any company in the environmental protection or sustainable energy sector. Everyone wants to be a leader in the new technologies that will drive this "sustainable" century. In keeping with this support for new-wave industries, almost every government is cloaking itself in the guise of a committed environmentalist. Each can feel the public pressure, and has at last woken up to the economic opportunities that will occur if we want to "save the planet." It is a new, shared morality, and it will underpin much of the Age of Selfish Altruism.

Perhaps the most sensible summary of the steps that are necessary to achieve sustainability is contained in the Earth Charter that is the product of a decade long, worldwide, cross-cultural dialogue on common goals and values. It began as a United Nations initiative, and was finally completed in 2002:

> The Earth Charter is a declaration of fundamental ethical principles for building a just, sustainable, and peaceful global society in the twenty-first century.
>
> The Earth Charter is centrally concerned with the transition to sustainable ways of living and sustainable human development.
>
> Ecological integrity is one major theme. However, the Earth Charter recognizes that the goals of ecological protection, the eradication of poverty, equitable economic development, respect for human rights, democracy, and peace are interdependent and indivisible.
>
> It provides, therefore, a new, inclusive, integrated ethical framework to guide the transition to a sustainable future.
>
> Life often involves tensions between important values. This can mean difficult choices. However, we must find ways to harmonize diversity with unity, the exercise of freedom with the common good, short-term objectives with long-term goals. Every individual, family, organization, and community has a vital role to play.

The Earth Charter has 16 basic pillars and details can be found at: www.earthcharterinaction.org.

Big Trend #2: When is Enough, Enough?

6

Modern society will find no solution to the ecological problem unless it takes a serious look at its lifestyle.

—Pope John Paul II

In the Consumer Century, conspicuous consumption was a sign of success. Keeping up with the Joneses, or the Chans, or the Patels, was a social necessity. The bigger house, new car, latest household goods, and designer-label clothes, were all evidence of your success in life. Swanky possessions were proof that you were "going places" and getting ahead. They were powerful symbols for self-esteem. Huge industries grew up to cater to these needs, and satisfy the ego and lifestyle aspirations of newly affluent consumers. Status was further increased by the brands you bought, and the conspicuous wearing of a brand's logo.

This desire for self-amplification and increased status drove economies and created global brands and retail empires. The brands you wore and used showed your status in life and your importance in society. Brands showed what kind of person you were, and helped define your personality and character. The clothes you wore, the watch you sported, and the car you drove, all added up to the picture you wanted to display of your individual persona. Materialism was king. The old maxim that "nothing succeeds like success" was changed to "nothing succeeds like excess."

Three changes are now occurring:

- First, everyone can afford designer brands. They no longer demonstrate the unique affluence or individual style that they did in the past. When we see advertisements for "entry-level luxury" products, we know that "exclusive" designers have stretched their brands way too far. Author Nick Foulkes talks about the "commoditization of luxury" being oxymoronic. Luxury should be exclusive and not for everyone, but many brands have simply become badges that are available to anyone with a couple of hundred dollars.

- Second, how many clothes, cars, televisions, fridges, and so on does a person need? The expectation that consumers will continue to acquire consumer goods with the same regularity and abandon seems highly unlikely. Even Anna Wintour, the editor-in-chief of *Vogue*, recently acknowledged that the culture of excess was winding down, and there is a new emphasis on "quality and longevity and things that really last."

- Third, there are clear signs that consumers in developed economies are moving beyond self-esteem toward "self-actualization." This is very much related to looking for more emotionally satisfying experiential and moral undertakings. The current economic downturn is reinforcing these new attitudes and rapidly moving people towards simpler, more meaningful lives and "responsible values." This is a trend that will permanently change purchase patterns in the future as we enter a new era of "post-consumerism."

New York communications agency Porter Novelli published a trend report in 2009 that identified new consumer behavior as a result of the economic crisis. At the top of Porter's list is "value and values." It believes that the lust for money will gradually wane in favor of new values such as stability, sustainability, and peace of mind. Porter predicts consumers will look beyond mere consumption. "We all have enough stuff; it's not where our heads are any more," said Marian Salzman, a Porter partner who is a recognized trend guru. "We're going to value a lot of things more, and not buy stuff we don't need."

"The era of conspicuous consumption is over," said Andy Bond, head of Wal-Mart's UK Asda subsidiary.

There is an increasing trend toward authenticity and craftsmanship that offer lasting value, rather than ostentation and flashy fashion. People are looking for better-made, tailored products that provide a deeper sense of satisfaction, rather than simply increasing self-esteem. Consumers are becoming more discerning, and are trading in old luxury brands for new luxury standards. Old luxury was driven by the need to be recognized, and success was demonstrated through shows of opulence and affluence. Old luxury demanded that you not only buy the best, but be seen to buy the best. So brand names had to be flashed and flaunted. What you wore, what you consumed, and what you drove were critical marks of old luxury.

In Asia, for example, the brands that were central to old luxury were Mercedes, Rolex, and Hennessy XO or Johnny Walker Black Label. No self-respecting entrepreneur or businessman would be seen without them. The wives of businessmen headed to the most expensive fashion shops and any "bling" jewelry store that would treat them like a goddess and deliver maximum flash.

Old luxury and self-esteem are inextricably interconnected. They are all about possessions and "look at me." New luxury is much more about "self-actualization," and the desire to make the most of life through experience, learning, and enjoyment. New luxury is less about possessions and more about taking time for yourself: going to a spa, having an adventure, taking an eco-lifestyle vacation, and belonging to a community dedicated to achieving new goals. The consumer goods that new luxury acquires are more understated and have authentic value, not just transient fashion and trendiness.

Consumer research recently undertaken for DeBeers Diamonds indicated that consumers were moving away from obvious displays of wealth, and toward products that were more specifically tailored to their needs. These changing values have also been spotted by the media. *Newsweek* magazine produced a special issue entitled "The Case for Luxury," which said, "The savvy shopper buys less, but spends more in hard times." This was reflected in a very good piece by Jonathan Tepperman about how "luxury lies not in how much stuff we have, but in how well it's made, and how highly we value it." His article goes on to eloquently say, "People are trading excess for excellence, superficiality for substance." He quotes a "flight to quality," as Louis Vuitton, Hermès, and other high-end brands enjoyed strong sales in early 2009 while most trendy and mid-range retailers were suffering badly in the economic downturn.

Articles in a wide range of publications have attempted a new definition of prestige and luxury as the evidence piles up that consumer perspectives are changing. In the *Robb Report*, Queen Elizabeth's nephew, the designer David Linley says, "The old meaning of luxury—all sorts of material things—needs to be re-evaluated. Real luxury is about attention to detail and the thought process behind it. It also depends on how you live your life. Luxury to me is having a bit of time off. All sorts of simple pleasures are now regarded as luxury." Another article in *Town & Country* decries "false luxury" in the age of mass consumption, and is appalled with the vulgarity of opulence and excess. "[Real] luxury is the coat or dress that has been made with the kind of attention to the details of cloth and color and cut and stitching that to wear it magically raises the spirits."

A study by ad agency JWT found that 85 percent of Americans surveyed in 2008 agreed with the statement "I am inclined to buy less stuff." So it does seem highly likely that sales volumes in many categories of consumer goods may decline, as changing attitudes are making consumers more careful and cautious about what they buy and why they are buying it. However, sales value may remain the same or greater, as people will likely be prepared to pay money more for lasting, real quality. Critical sales factors for the twenty-first century will be quality not quantity, and values not just value.

Manufacturers and retailers may therefore have to prepare for change. The old business model of ever-increasing volumes and lower prices will need to adapt to a more value-added, lower-volume, ethically minded marketplace. Until very recently, factories around the world have been producing ever-increasing quantities of consumer goods on the basis that demand will continue to increase.

Chinese Production

Perhaps the most notable example of massive productive capacity being created to satisfy burgeoning consumer demand is China. China's economy has enjoyed staggering growth largely on the back of consumer demand in the US and other developed countries for the products it manufactures in greater and greater quantities. Several years ago, one of the large international management consultants produced what I thought was a brilliant model for growth in the China market itself. It was a bell curve (again!) in which average household income formed the horizontal axis of the chart (see figure 6.1). The vertical index represented volume. As income gradually increased, so the number of people in China who could afford a particular product was indicated by a rise up the bell curve. So, for example, a radio was affordable with a household income of only $100 per month. As more and more people started to earn more than $100 a month, so the potential for sales of radios grew dramatically—not in a slow, gradual way, but enormous growth as tens of millions of households all started to earn more than $100 a month. Television purchases would demand an income of $300 per month, fridges $400 a month, and so on.

Using this model, it was possible to map future demand for a whole series of product categories as the economy expanded and average income grew. The steep side of the bell curve shows how quickly product adoption occurs. Within China itself, millions of new consumers have been created as household incomes rose rapidly, but product saturation is often achieved surprisingly quickly, and replacement markets generate much slower sales and lower volumes. Therefore Chinese manufacturers quickly

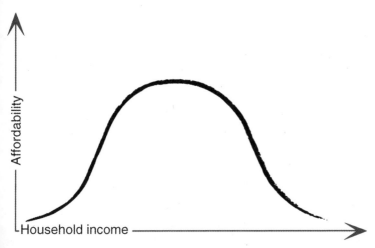

Figure 6.1 China bell curve

sought overseas outlets for their products, and foreign buyers stimulated the production of an ever increasing array of goods.

In the face of the current global economic slow-down, China seems to have done an excellent job of stimulating domestic consumer demand to provide a sales outlet for the thousands of domestic manufacturers whose export markets have dried up. However, there is an assumption that once Chinese domestic demand is saturated over the next couple of years, the global markets will again be able to consume Chinese manufactured goods in the same way as before. This may be true in the short term, because there has to be some pent-up demand, but longer term the changing mindset of consumers in developed markets will start to affect what they buy and the way they buy.

Economist Stephen Roach was quoted as saying "there is evidence to believe that the capitulation of the American consumer has only just begun." Ajay Chhibber at the UN Development Program agrees, "The model where you stimulate and then go back to the old days is gone."

China will not be able to keep ramping up production and assume that overseas markets will soak up its manufactured goods.

Emerging markets may still enjoy growing sales as a new generation of affluent, aspiring consumers emerges. But developed countries are much more likely to see flat or declining volumes because of changing values and aging populations. Business models throughout the twentieth century were built on a premise of ever increasing annual sales. In this new century, many companies will need to consider flat or declining sales volumes to be the norm, and any growth at all to be a real achievement.

New Aspirations

The current financial crisis is making people ask themselves, "what do I actually *need* to buy?" There is clear evidence that people are much more conscious about their spending habits and are consuming less wastefully. The habit of "trading up" every couple of years is likely to change significantly, and will become a thing of the past.

Aspirations may also be changing. In the past people aspired to bigger, better, and more. Their self-worth and self-esteem were largely measured by their possessions. There is evidence now that aspirations are shifting away from possessions and material gain toward a simpler, more meaningful lifestyle. This is due to the combination of changing personal needs, economic crisis, and aging baby-boom population. Affluent people are reassessing their aspirations and looking to find something more meaningful in their life than the "fame and fortune" goals of their youth.

It may also be due to a new mindset, especially among younger people, who realize that rapid economic growth and continual consumption are simply not sustainable. Others may simply want to drop out of the "rat race" and live a more fulfilling life. Whatever the reason may be, it is clear that change is happening.

A 2008 survey by JWT revealed that two-thirds of Americans would prefer to have a job that allowed them to "give back" to society. More than half admitted to thinking more about "the road not taken" lately. They also agreed that there are times "I wish I could have an entirely different life," and wished they could make an entire career change. The object of their reflections and introspection was the desire for a simpler life. Half the people in the survey felt that their life had become too complex, with not enough time to do everything that needed doing. A quarter of the respondents said that they were already opting for a simpler life by spending more time with their family. Only 10 percent of people who were questioned said they didn't want a simpler life. These changing aspirations were all in the context of most respondents in the study expecting their financial situation to improve in the future, so it wasn't simply a response to lower incomes. It was a genuine desire to add a new dimension to their lives that was more meaningful than constant consumption and a search for greater self-esteem.

The whole consumer mindset seems to be changing, and this may even change the definition of a "consumer." The word "consume" is based on the Latin *consumere*, which literally means "intensive taking." Dictionaries define "consume" in several ways, many of which harken back to the word's original roots:

To expend; use up

To waste; squander

To destroy totally; ravage.

So our current understanding of consuming being a friendly, positive word that relates to eating or buying may well drift back to once again being a word relating to waste or damage. Consumerism is in danger of becoming a dirty word as it increasingly implies ostentation, wastefulness, and to some extent greed and selfishness. Consumerism too often relates to excessive volume and selfish buying, especially in connection with food or clothing or consumer goods. Old habits are changing quickly as we enter a post-consumer era that is more conscious of community rather than status, value instead of indulgence, and basic needs not bling.

These attitudes are beginning to mesh with concerns about the environment, as the ecological cost of manufacture and the environmental damage that occurs is becoming part of the buying consideration. Society is becoming much more concerned about what it buys and why. A new post-consumer mindset is being created, which will be much more concerned about real values and more sensible purchasing. The old conspicuous consumerism of the past will not aggressively reassert itself globally.

In many Asian countries, where the standard of living continues to rise and many people still aspire to the finer things in life, twentieth-century-style consumerism will continue for a decade or two. But in affluent Western markets all the evidence is pointing to a fundamental change of behavior caused by a more frugal and pragmatic mindset.

There must be more to life than having everything!
—Maurice Sendak, author

Big Trend #3: Changing Demographics: The "Silver Revolution"

7

Aging seems to be the only available way to live a long life.

—Kitty O'Neill Collins, author

We are about to enter a geriatric world! The twenty-first century may well be defined as the Silver Century as older people come to form the majority of many populations, and dominate the economy and government policy. The global average age will rise significantly as birth rates decline and people live longer. Most European countries and several Asian countries are already feeling the first effects of a rapidly aging populace. This will become much, much more apparent over the next few decades as older people far outnumber children and teens in the overall population of many nations.

We have lived all of our lives in societies with young populations, where marketers have targeted teens, young adults, and new families as their best prospects. Over the years I have become used to clients defining their media target group as "all people 18–35," or adults "18–45." When consumers approached 50, they were written off as being no longer important, except for product categories such as denture cleansers, incontinency pads, and various medicines. For the past 50 years we have also heard about the problems of rapid population growth, and have become almost inured to stories and charity appeals recounting the complications that this has caused, from poverty to urban unrest, and famine to slum cities. There have been repeated warnings that the world cannot tolerate such a rapid headcount increase, and we have come to assume that population growth is a problem that will never be easily solved.

However, the situation has been changing very markedly over the past couple of decades, and a *declining* population is one of the biggest issues facing many developed countries. "Negative" birthrates for the past few decades are already creating population decline in major countries, and the world may finally stop growing within the next 40–50 years.

A result of slowing global growth rates is that the world's population will become a lot older. The proportion of children in the overall population will decline, as the number of aged people is already growing rapidly. The next five decades will see a massive aging of the world population. The number of people over 80 years of age will rise a staggering 500 percent.

Many developed countries already have almost a quarter of their population over 60 years of age, and this will rise to more than one-third over the next 40 years. So one person in three will be a "pensioner!" The twenty-first century will be as much about older people as the twentieth century was a celebration of youth. The rapid aging of populations isn't a temporary "baby boom" phenomenon; it is a long-term trend that will create a global society very much dominated by older people. The median age will be 38 years in 2050, compared to just 29 today.

The normal pyramid of age distribution that we have all become accustomed to will rapidly invert as old people come to outnumber young children. This will put enormous pressure on social systems and economies, and cause consumer buying habits to change radically. An aged population has very different attitudes, values, and lifestyle from those of younger individuals and families, which will create a whole range of economic and social challenges. The buying habits and consumerism of a country that has a young and growing population will contrast greatly with those of a nation where most of its people are well into the second half of their lives.

Many people love statistics. Sadly, I'm not one of them. However, some of the data relating to population were very surprising to me when I started to dig into the reasons for consumer aging, and absolutely fascinating. I really had no idea of the tsunami-like changes that are occurring, and how different the "silver" twenty-first century will be to the youthful, "swinging" twentieth century that most of us grew up in. The comedy program *Monty Python's Flying Circus* had a sketch that parodied the Hell's Angels biker gang. It featured a group of silver-haired old ladies swaggering down the street shouldering people aside while acting mean and tough. They wore black leather jackets with the words "Hell's Grannies" emblazoned on the back. The sketch was a mock documentary and the commentator recounted how these aggressive oldies were terrifying their local community. The old-aged delinquents were responsible for bullying, shoplifting, and worst of all—not paying their bus fares when traveling at peak times. The sketch was hilarious, but may well have been inadvertently prophetic.

Even if populations and economies were growing strongly, most developed countries would find that continuing the current system of "entitlement" to pensions and free health care impossible to sustain as the baby boomers retire. However, many developed countries now have a declining population and very little economic growth, so "entitlement reform," as the IMF calls it, will be necessary in the very near future.

The Twentieth-Century Population Boom

The world first provided accommodation for a billion people in 1804. It took 50,000–200,000 years to reach that first billion, depending on your starting point for modern humans. Just 103 years later, we had reached two billion. Since then, things have accelerated greatly. Starting in the 1950s, the world has been adding an extra billion humans to its total population

Population (in billions)	1	2	3	4	5	6	7
Years	1804	1927	1959	1974	1987	1999	2012
Years elapsed		123	32	14.75	13.25	12.25	12.33	13

Figure 7.1 Time for each billion increase in global population

approximately *every 14 years*. The global population topped six billion by the end of 1999, and will hit seven billion about 2012 (see figure 7.1).

The human population is expected to grow to about nine billion souls by 2050, and then it *may* reach the top of its bell curve and flatten out at that level. There are many different forecasts of world population growth, but they all agree on the key elements (see figure 7.2):

- Europe's population is already at the beginning of a gradual, long-term decline.

- Asia's population growth will moderate significantly, and may begin to flatten out from 2030–40 onward, in large part due to declining populations in Japan and China, and declining birth rates elsewhere.

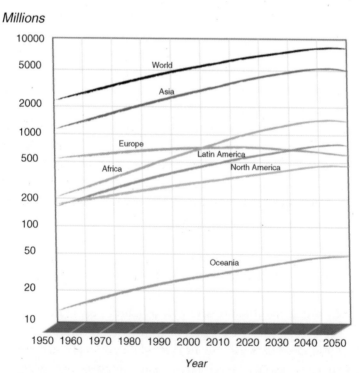

Figure 7.2 Global population

- Middle Eastern and African populations will continue to grow massively unless the birth rates are moderated through new economic affluence, or death rates increase through the "Malthusian" effects of disease, famine, or war.

Why Population Has Increased

The enormous increase in the world's population over the past 50 years has been a function of several factors, but the most important have been affluence, health care, and agriculture. Increasing national wealth allowed many countries to achieve improvements in sanitary facilities, with clean water access, proper drainage and sewage facilities, garbage disposal, heat, and light for individual homes. Modern housing with "all mod cons" has now come to be seen as a human right, rather than a privilege.

Discoveries and innovations in health care over the past century have been remarkable, and will continue to provide some of the most important and fundamental changes in the twenty-first century. The developments of antiseptics and antibiotics and the discovery of penicillin have saved millions of lives. Entire diseases, such as smallpox and polio, have been either eradicated or severely curtailed through inoculations and vaccinations. Better medical care and improved diets have reduced infant mortality and extended life. Recently, the mapping of the human genome has revealed a new world of genetic opportunities, along with the many moral dilemmas that this creates. Finally, the Green Revolution allowed more intensive farming techniques and better crop yields to meet the food needs of a rapidly growing population.

All these factors contributed to the rapid and sustained growth of the planet's population. However, although the number of people on Earth will continue to grow over the near future, the *rate of growth* has been declining for some time. After peaking in the mid-1960s, the yearly rate of population growth has consistently declined from a high of 2.2 percent per annum to less than 1 percent today. The rate of growth of the population is forecast to continue to decline until some global population equilibrium is reached about 2050, when forecasts show negligible global growth rates (see figure 7.3).

The Importance of Birthrates

A critical moderating factor in the rate of population growth is the reduced birthrate that occurs with increasing wealth. Fertility rates are inversely proportional to wealth and the associated cost of living, so

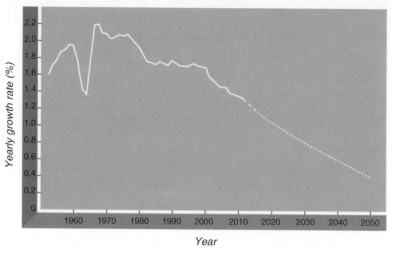

Figure 7.3 Rate of global population increase
Source: UN

broadly speaking the more affluent a country, the lower the birth rate. This is a function of several factors, including:

- career women marrying at an older age and having children later in life

- higher divorce rates

- the cost of rearing and educating children

- the lack of social structure to help working parents

- most importantly of all, there is no *need* to have lots of children to provide income and support for their parents, thanks to pension plans, government social programs, and higher savings.

Children therefore become a "lifestyle option" rather than an economic necessity in developed countries.

The evidence clearly indicates that as a country develops economically, the birth rate tends to drop (see figure 7.4). So poor countries in Africa have the highest birthrates, and highly developed countries (especially those with a high cost of living) have some of the lowest. I'm not sure that Niger is proud of its position as the most fertile country on earth, with an average birth rate (2000–05) of 7.45, but it certainly is impressive. Contrast that with Germany at 1.35, Japan at 1.29, and Hong Kong, which at 0.94 has the lowest birthrate in the world.

Hong Kong is densely populated, very affluent, and has some of the highest housing costs on earth. Living accommodation is cramped, and raising children is logistically difficult and very expensive. All these

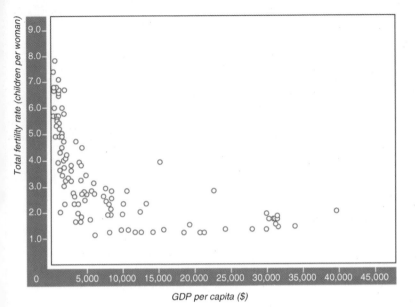

Figure 7.4 Total fertility rate vs. GDP per capita
Source: CIA—The World Factbook

factors combine to limit most families to having a single child or none at all. Singapore, South Korea, and Japan all have similar economic and social situations with resulting very low birth rates.

As a function of differing economic development and socio-political environments, the rates of fertility and associated population growth vary widely across the world (see figure 7.5).

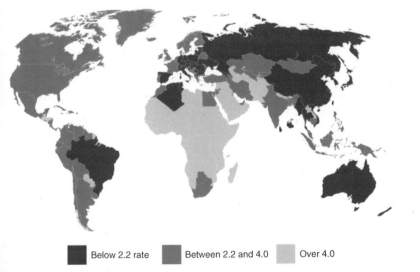

    ■ Below 2.2 rate   ■ Between 2.2 and 4.0   □ Over 4.0

Figure 7.5 Global fertility rates

The world's overall population is still growing, but the vast differences in fertility are now delivering a negative growth rate in most developed countries. The UN estimates that the average global fertility rate will fall from 2.56 children per woman in 2005 to 2.02 in 2045–50. Generally, a fertility rate of approximately 2.2 is assumed to be the population replacement rate in a developed country. So any nation with a lower fertility rate will begin to suffer population decline, unless supplemented by immigration.

As can be seen in figure 7.5, most developed and many developing countries now have a "negative birth rate," that is, a birth rate below 2.2, and will eventually feel population decline, but it will require a complete "lifecycle" to occur. The conversion of a "negative birth rate" into significant population decline can take several decades or close to the full lifespan of a generation. People in developed countries are living longer, so extended life often masks the impact of a low birth rate for some extra time.

The death rate has to consistently exceed the birth rate before population decline occurs. For example, the dramatic effect of the one-child policy in China, which began in 1979, will not convert into population decline until 2040 and beyond. After 2015, the number of workers in China will gradually decline, and the elderly as a proportion of the population will grow noticeably. However, the *total population* will not begin to decline until 2030 onwards, when those first children born under the "one child per family" policy begin to pass away and the continuing low fertility rate begins to have a clear effect (see table 7.1). So it will take 50–60 years, or almost the lifespan of a generation, for the effect of a negative birthrate to actually result in declining population.

Table 7.1 Population of China

Year	1950	2000	2015	2025	2050
Population of China (millions)	554	1,275	1,410	1,441	1,392

Source: UN estimates

Changes in Europe

This same phenomenon of impending population decline is unfolding in many other developed and developing countries, primarily in Europe. Most dramatically, Russia, Germany, Poland and several other European

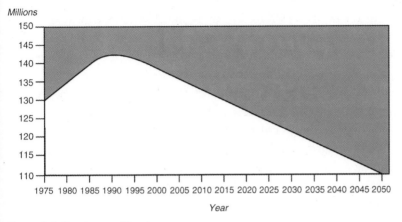

Figure 7.6 Population of Russia
Source: OECD

states *already have declining populations* after decades of negative birth rates. Russia's population began to decline in the early 1990s and accelerated downward as the new millennium began. Over the first 12 years of life of the Russian Federation, from its creation in 1992 until 2004, its population declined by 3 percent. From a peak of nearly 149 million Russians, only 142 million survive today. At one point in the 1990s, Russia reported 160 deaths for every 100 births.

The UN is forecasting that Russia will suffer a decline of 840,000 people per year, which is equivalent to 21 million over the period 2000–25. The country's population is expected to continue to slide down to 110 million by 2050 (see figure 7.6).

Russia has suffered a triple whammy to its population: low birth rates, high death rates (one of the lowest average lifespans in Europe), and emigration. Alcohol abuse and the wrenching change of lifestyle as the country went through massive market reforms, created high levels of uncertainty which are not conducive to either long life or childrearing. Recent economic expansion, high gas and mineral prices, and significant foreign investment have all "disguised" the population decline as workers shift from state to private industry and people move to new geographies to find employment. But with increasing stabilization of the economy, the impact of a reducing workforce and aging population will be felt much more acutely.

In the rest of Europe, major population changes are also occurring which may have considerable political effect. Eurostat is predicting that Germany will fall from being the EU's most populous state with more than 82 million people to third largest with 71 million in 2060. There will be a drop of 10 million in Germany's population, equivalent to an almost

14 percent decline, and it has already begun. Poland will have a similar decline from 38 million to 31 million Poles. Conversely, the number of British will increase by 15 million, and it will replace Germany as Europe's most populous state.

Because seats in the European Parliament are related to the size of a state, some redistribution is likely in favor of Britain, France, and Spain, which all have rising populations. Conversely, Germany, Poland, and many Eastern European states with declining populations may lose parliamentary seats and the accompanying political influence.

Effects of Immigration

Many countries have attempted to counteract negative birthrates through immigration. Britain and France, for example, have encouraged significant immigration, and as a result have growing populations, although this gain has been achieved at the cost of cultural homogeneity. The trick to effective immigration is to forge a melting pot of ethnicities and culture and religious freedom into a single national identity. This has proven very difficult for most European countries to achieve in the first or even second generations of immigrants, and inevitably causes civil unrest in some shape or another.

And before our American readers feel overly virtuous, I would like to remind them of the "No Irish" hiring policies of the nineteenth century; negro emancipation and the subsequent fight for equality by blacks; Jewish and Italian ghettos; current Hispanic problems; and many other "melting pot" issues of the past 200 years. Immigration is difficult, but it is also necessary for many developed countries to continue to grow. The US, Canada, and Australia, for example, have long encouraged immigration and are familiar with the difficulties that come with cultural and linguistic assimilation. However, European countries that have only recently encouraged large-scale immigration have suffered some severe cultural problems for which they were unprepared. Immigrants with different religions, races and mores have created fear and rejection from the more culturally homogenous indigenous population in many European countries. And the immigrants themselves often feel that they are treated as second-class citizens in their new country of choice. The recent immigrant riots in France mirrored those that occurred in Britain a few years ago. Spain, Italy, and even ultra-liberal Holland are having enormous issues absorbing different immigrant groups with different clothing, religion and social mores.

An interesting example of one of the social problems of immigration can be seen in the UK where the children of the recent immigrant inflow are now inadvertently generating problems in the education system. In 2009, one in seven British primary schoolchildren did not speak English as a first language. Almost a million children currently in primary and secondary schools across the UK speak English as a second language, and in some areas this amounts to 70 percent of 4–11 year olds. In one school in east London, only one-quarter of all pupils were native English speakers, and the other three-quarters of the schoolchildren spoke 56 different languages as their mother tongue.

Immigration in Asia

Disturbing the homogenous nature of the country is the key reason why Asian countries facing population decline have been most unwilling to open their doors to immigrants. Japan has very little immigration as it continues to be very xenophobic about foreigners. Second-generation Koreans, for example, who were actually born and educated in Japan, still don't have Japanese citizenship. They are classified as "resident aliens," and any attempt to pretend they are actually Japanese can have dire social and employment consequences if their "true identity" is discovered. Japan's attitudes to foreigners can be seen at the immigration counters when you arrive. There are two sets of counters: one for Japanese, and the other for "Aliens." Although most of us find being called an "alien" quite amusing, particularly in the past when various Spielberg movies were playing, it does accurately reflect how the Japanese see people from other countries. The government of Japan is now appealing to ethnic Japanese who live in other countries to "come home" to the country of their roots.

Although Koreans suffer discrimination in Japan, Korea itself is similarly xenophobic, as is China, which is deeply distrustful of those who are not ethnically Han. Try getting a Thai or Vietnamese passport: it is virtually impossible if you were not born in the country. Hong Kong and Singapore solve the problem of population decline by bringing in foreign workers or immigrants from China, or ethnic Chinese from Malaysia and Indonesia. However, even in the very cosmopolitan and multiculturally sensitive Singapore, there is constant criticism of the bad behavior and habits of "mainland Chinese" immigrants who have difficulty settling into a more orderly and polite society. So even immigrants who have the same ethnicity, language, and religion can have difficulties fitting into the social mores of a new country.

Japan: A Graying Nation

I don't want to get this narrative bogged down with boring statistics, but it is worthwhile looking at some key charts relating to the Japanese population, because they offer a view of the future that is completely unprecedented in our lifetimes.

Japan is at the beginning of an accelerating population decline that will see the number of Japanese drop by half over the next 100 years (see figure 7.7). During this time, Japan will increasingly become a geriatric society, with far more older people than younger. This will produce enormous social and economic strains, and completely change the consumption patterns of the country.

The number of deaths is now greater than the number of births, and this situation will continue as far as can be seen into the future. Japan is doing little to reverse this situation, and has one of the weakest "social contracts" to encourage childbirth of any developed nation.

The Japanese government has failed to provide the same social provisions and tax incentives that are common in most European nations now facing the same low birthrates and challenge of depopulation. Paid absence from work after childbirth for women is simply not generous enough, and extended time off for men is culturally unacceptable in Japan.

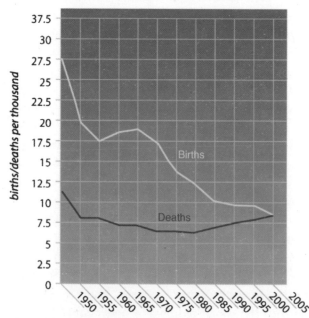

Figure 7.7 Japanese birth and death rate
Source: Japanese Statistics Bureau

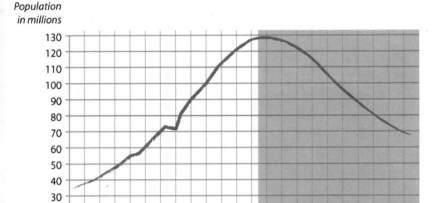

Population
in millions

Figure 7.8 Japanese population from 1870 to 2100 (projected)

Government-sponsored tax breaks and other financial incentives have always been inadequate to encourage more child births, and still are.

The result is that in 2008, the Japanese Health Ministry estimated the population fell by 51,000 as the number of deaths hit a record 1.14 million, which is the highest since the government began compiling the data in 1947, and the number of births totaled only 1.09 million. This trend will accelerate in the future as Japan begins to de-populate from 130 million people towards 65 million by the end of the century (see figure 7.8).

With low birthrates and long lifespans, Japan's shrinking population is aging more quickly than that of any other economic power. Already, more than 20 percent of Japan's population is 65 years or older, and this is forecast to rise to a staggering 40 percent over the next four decades!

The result of ever fewer children and ever more old people is that the "normal" population pyramid, which has a large, wide, youthful base and tapers to a narrow old-age peak, will almost reverse. We have become accustomed to the "normal" pyramid of age distribution, and we take for granted that it will always be like this. Not in Japan. Already in 2007, the pyramid has become more like a solid tree trunk. By 2050, it will become more of an inverted pyramid (see figure 7.9).

To understand the effect that this will create, imagine living in Tokyo, where the proportion of elderly people will reach 25 percent of its total population in 2015. A quarter of all people in this giant city will be "old age pensioners," or "silver citizens." And it will continue to get

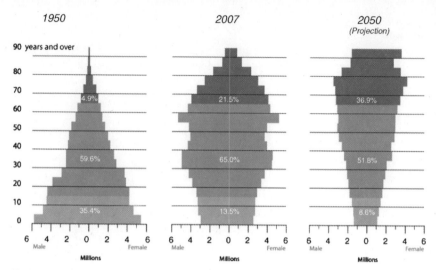

Figure 7.9 Japanese population age distribution

"grayer" as the average age keeps inexorably rising. Living in a geriatric society is already causing some frustrations for younger people in Tokyo, as everything from public transport to retailers and restaurants caters to older customers.

It is patently obvious that the aspirations and consumption patterns of a society where the population is declining and the average age is approaching 50 years are markedly different from those of a growing, younger population. Japan can therefore give us a glimpse of the situation that a declining population creates, and the effect that a geriatric society has on attitudes, values, and behavior. This will draw a picture of what many European and Asian countries will face in the near future, and provide some greater insight into the emerging Age of Selfish Altruism.

The Impact of Old Age on the Japanese Economy

Since the economic bubble burst in 1990, Japan has had insignificant economic growth despite enjoying interest rates at almost zero for the past two decades. The country has seen price deflation for most of those years despite continual and massive government stimulus programs. The reasons seem pretty obvious to me. In the 1990s, Japanese workers faced unemployment for the first time in their lives. Until the "bubble" burst, people in postwar Japan had only seen continuing growth in their standard of living, increasing affluence, and absolute job security.

This paradigm shifted in the 1990s when the property boom came to an end, and banks were faced with horrific toxic loans on their books.

Pretty much the same situation as the US faces today. Since 1990, Japan has enjoyed very little growth, and most of the past 15 years have seen deflation in prices, which has put further downward pressure on every part of its economy.

It is popular to blame the Japanese government for not cleaning up bank debts more aggressively and rapidly. There is also criticism of mistimed interest rate movement and ineffective stimulus packages filled with unnecessary infrastructure programs. Japan has a lot of "bridges to nowhere" and highways leading to no place. There may be some truth in all of these criticisms leveled at the government, but I would offer only one proverb in defense of the Japanese policy makers: "You can lead a horse to water, but you can't make it drink."

Those Japanese workers who were aged 40 or above in 1990 became very aware that their jobs were on the line, and they needed to think about security and their pensions! A very large proportion of Japanese workers fell into that age group, and even more do now. Interest rates at close to zero offered little inducement to spend. I would argue that they had the opposite effect, because savings accounts gained virtually no interest.

House prices declined or remained flat at best, and the collapsed stock market failed to recover to anywhere near its old levels. So people couldn't find a way to increase their net worth. This would make them more conservative in their spending patterns, and focus on savings.

When your focus is on long-term security and the health of your pension plan, the last thing you want to do is go out and spend, no matter how low the interest rates. Japanese baby boomers suddenly came face to face with the fact they may not have enough pension money to last them the rest of their days. Consumption patterns changed and the prospect of forced, early retirement focused the mind on items of durable, lasting value, rather than short-term profligacy or the sheer joy of shopping.

Ad agency JWT has an "Anxiety Index," which constantly measures how anxious people are in a broad range of countries. The Japanese top the list as the world's most anxious people. The Russians are the second-most anxious, followed by the Americans. This may be partly due to older workers in the US now facing the same dilemma of imminent retirement as Japanese employees were faced with more than a decade ago. Baby boomers in the US have just seen their pension plans decimated and the value of their homes plummet. No matter what the government offers, they are most unlikely to become conspicuous consumers ever again.

The key difference from Japan is that the US has a much younger, growing population, thanks to high levels of immigration with greater fertility rates. So the increased conservatism of the baby boomers can be partly offset by the retail enthusiasm of younger consumers once their confidence returns. This is very different than Japan, where older workers and retirees are about to become the most dominant part of society. Japanese consumer goods don't have a burgeoning younger group of high-spending new families who will replace their increasingly conservative parents.

I'm not an economist, but the implications for Japan seem fairly obvious:

- Retail sales volume will gradually decline and the product mix will change.

- Real estate prices and GNP will remain soft or undergo long term decline.

- Savings rates will decline significantly as the number of retirees increases.

Japan has suffered a deflationary environment over the past two decades, and it seems logical that this is likely to remain so despite many attempts by the government to reverse it. Japan therefore offers us a vision of the "catastrophic" economic effect of an aging population. Spending patterns change . . . forever.

Once the comfort of rising house prices, a growing pension plan, and job security is threatened, older consumers focus on protecting their assets, not buying new status symbols. If a population overall is aging, this pension-protecting mentality will slow the entire economy, even without any economic shock. The absence of new young consumers to take up the consumption slack, means that the total economy suffers and low levels of growth and deflation are inevitable. Several countries face this same scenario. The biggest are China, Russia, Germany, Italy, and Poland.

It can be argued by environmentalists that continuous growth is a key problem for the planet and in fact a reduction of GDPs is a healthy thing. This may well be true for the environment and the health of the world's ecosystems. But I can tell you, as a businessman, that managing decline is a lot more painful and difficult than managing growth. Knowing that every year revenues will decline, and at a faster rate than staff reductions, means some very difficult decisions have to be made. Priorities need to be established, and some very unpopular decisions made.

Japan is already finding this out. The amount of care required for older, less mobile people is becoming a major issue. Health services are becoming stretched, and staffing problems are emerging everywhere. This is why Japan is putting such efforts into robotics. It may well become a nation of robots if current demographics continue! Many businesses are now realizing the importance of employee retention in a country where the number of available workers is set to decline dramatically. So women are becoming much more treasured, and companies are finally offering more generous child-related leave, or re-employment whenever they are ready to return to the workforce after their children have grown older.

Interestingly, elderly care programs are also starting to be provided by businesses, as the onus on females to take care of aging family members is preventing them from taking on a full-time job. So companies are offering the equivalent of child-care programs for the elderly. Granny-sitters to look after mother-in-law, and the opposite of kindergartens, whatever that is, for oldsters? This is surely a sign of things to come! As countries age, day care for the elderly will become more prevalent than child care.

China

Given China's importance to the twenty-first century, it is worth spending a few moments to understand the impact of the demographic changes that will occur in that country over the next few years. China has extraordinary issues, which are not well known, but will have enormous domestic implications, and eventually a global impact.

China's one-child policy, which began in 1979, will result in a declining population from about 2040 onward. India will overtake China as the world's most populous nation a few years before that time. The statistics that face China are quite extraordinary:

- China's working population is currently growing to just over a massive billion workers when the number peaks in 2015. It will then decline by 23 percent over the following 35 years. That's about 250 million workers leaving China's workforce!
- By 2050, there will be 438 million Chinese above the age of 60.
- In 2005, there were 100 working people supporting every 16 people over the age of 60. By 2050, the 100 people employed will need to support 61 people over the age of 60.
- Growth in the labor force has been adding approximately 1.8 percent to GDP growth over the past three decades. By the 2030s, the decline in the labor force will chop 0.7 percent off annual GDP growth.

The implications for China are enormous. The country will lose its low-cost manufacturing edge as the working population declines and there is increasing competition for employees. India, Vietnam, and other populous nations with expanding workforces will take over the low-cost manufacturing mantle from the People's Republic.

China will need to add value to its manufacturing and service industries, and perhaps this is one reason the government is actively supporting new industries such as electric cars and solar energy development. Fashion, design, and entertainment industries are blossoming in China, as are a myriad of entrepreneurial businesses in many New Age sectors. The country will need to stay on this course, as its days as the world's low-cost producer will soon come to an end.

Big Trend #4: The Power of Collaboration, Community, and Consensus

8

Friendship is the only cement that will ever hold the world together.
—Woodrow Wilson, US president

We can see from the three big trends previously discussed that a major shift in values is occurring globally. Environmentalism is creating a new set of ethics, which become more deeply entrenched as the urgent need for sustainability becomes apparent. The shift toward responsible consumption is creating a new type of post-consumer, who has different values and is searching for real value.

The rapidly growing, youthful population of the twentieth century is transforming into a more mature global populace, which has very different needs and values from younger communities. All these major trends are creating a new set of values that are coalescing and feeding off each other. The ethics of the environmental movement are affecting buying behavior. Buying behavior is being further affected by an aging population, which is in turn spearheading some of the drive for sustainability. Each trend is complemented by the others. What is giving every one of these three big trends a more powerful momentum is a final trend: *the new power of collaboration, community, and consensus.*

We could argue that collaboration, community, and consensus are three minor trends, rather than one big one, but I think that they all stem from the same basic attitudes and behavior. A recent JWT Trendletter was titled "The Collective Consciousness," and it found that "People are pooling resources, sharing ideas and coordinating actions as never before. This trend is being fostered by the desire and ability to join communities; the ease with which Web technology allows people to communicate, exchange ideas and organize collectively; and the growing realization that large scale problems need large scale, collectively driven solutions."

This "collective consciousness" is adding further impetus to the changing values of the twenty-first century like three strong winds of opinion combining into a hurricane of conviction. *Collaboration* will increasingly govern personal and business life as we find collective solutions to common problems. *Communal* activities based on shared values and common goals will dominate individual behavior and reinforce social groups and the family unit. *Consensus* will allow people to share ideas, create opinions, and generate mass movements that encourage more active engagement to change political and social policies.

These changes in behavior will eventually create a new morality, which is an almost nineteenth-century-style return to social responsibility, family values, and sense of duty.

The Power of Collaboration

Good design begins with honesty, asks tough questions, comes from collaboration and from trusting your intuition.
—Freeman Thomas, designer

Of all the behavioral trends in this century, collaboration will be the most important because it will influence and empower communities, companies, and countries. Real-time collaboration on a global scale has been enabled by the internet and new telecommunications facilities. As a result, collaboration has become an immensely powerful tool for business, politics, and individuals with similar interests or attitudes. In the past, the telephone created some degree of long-distance collaboration, but it was limited for a very long time by its one-to-one oral/aural function. Mobile phones set the pace for more widespread communication and collaboration through both written and oral facilities. However, it is the internet, and especially social networking sites, which have transformed interpersonal communication from one-to-one to one-to-millions.

Whether it is an individual communicating to just a select group of friends, or to anyone who wants to listen, the internet now has the technical ability to take one person's views and share it with millions of other people in seconds. Within minutes a point of view can be debated, and within an hour a mass movement can be formed. People with similar values, ethics, and attitudes can find each other and share opinions or plan action.

Geography, race, age, sex and religion are irrelevant because the internet is the great equalizer. Anyone who has access to the internet can share his or her opinions with an almost infinite number of other people. The result is that collaboration is being increasingly taken for granted in this online world we now live in. Whether it is simply planning a trip, discussing an issue, or joining a movement for change, we automatically involve others, some of whom we know, but very many others we don't. Although the most obvious manifestation of this collaboration is Facebook and other social networking sites, business and politics are rapidly grabbing the same online tools to engage with their audiences more directly.

Politicians are realizing the collaborative power of the internet, and the ability to reach out to thousands or millions of voters to solicit their views in a way previously only possible through personal contact. Film and music stars are staying in close personal contact with their fans through Twitter. Businesses are coming to understand that their customers can not only influence sales, but also contribute to the design of their company's products and services.

Collaborative, user-driven development will increasingly play a key role in the design and manufacture of products, and companies will be increasingly responsive to user feedback, opinions and ideas. Open-source manufacture will become standard operating procedure for companies who seek rapid and cost-efficient expansion. Collaboration will change how people work as well as how products are created.

The internet has provided a wide array of collaborative tools that are an integral part of the lifestyle of young people today in every part of the world. Social networking sites continue to grow, collaborative authoring is quite normal, social bookmarking expands horizons, and blogging or microblogging is part of everyday life. All these different tools are setting the tone for the collaborative twenty-first century. A vast number of people now share their likes, dislikes, opinions, and actions with their friends, colleagues, and anyone else who wants to know. This exposure of personal data, image, actions, and attitudes is pretty much the polar opposite of the "right to privacy," which was such a feature of the previous century. Invasion of privacy seems such a dated concept when it seems that everyone you know, and many you don't, are posting far more information about themselves than you actually ever wanted to know.

Bill Gates closed his Facebook account when 10,000 people per day wanted to be his friend. Despite Bill opting out, social networking will become even stronger in the future. At its peak levels of growth, Facebook was adding 50,000 new users around the world *every day*. Websites and social networks are springing up for people who want to share their news, opinions, attitudes, and actions with others who have common interests or relationships.

Word of Mouth

This has changed the way we "shop," and increasingly we search for the opinions of others before making any buying decision. Collaborative activity is now standard behavior in the purchase process, and a critical factor in the final decision. A poor rating or a series of negative comments by past buyers can kill any chance of a new sale. Positive ratings and satisfied comments from people already using a product or service will significantly increase the likelihood of purchase by new customers. *Word of mouth has never been more powerful than at present, and it can make or break businesses and brands.*

Companies need to monitor online opinions being expressed about them and their products. If they fail to do so, a stream of negative comments can impact a business before the company even understands what the problem is. A few years ago Engadget found that the "toughest bicycle security lock," called the Kryptonite Evolution 2000, could be opened with a Bic ballpoint pen. Its online posting joked that the pen was mightier than the lock, and beware of bicycle thieves armed with a Bic pen. This single story soon raced around the internet and concerned cyclists became very wary of the lock (which was soon modified). Before the internet, the discovery about a Bic pen being able to open a lock would have been limited to a few friends chatting, a letter to the company, or even a magazine item. The company could have taken action while most buyers and users remained unaware of this flaw in the lock's design.

The internet has changed all that. The speed at which a story can be posted, picked up and retransmitted to a million people can wreak havoc on a business almost before the company is aware of the problem. Businesses now have to take online feedback about their products very seriously indeed, because the negative opinions of a large number of detractors can irreversibly damage a brand.

Apple learned how to collaborate more effectively with its users after the damage to its business caused initially by a single consumer complaining about the screen of his iPod Nano becoming scratched very easily. The Nano user had failed to get an adequate response from Apple about this problem, so he posted his complaints on the internet. Others who had purchased the Nano agreed with his complaints and soon there was a serious online backlash against the company. Apple failed to respond quickly or adequately as the number of online complaints mounted and sales of the iPod Nano began to slide. Eventually, the company could see and feel the damage to its business that these disgruntled online complainants were causing. It couldn't simply ignore the problem and hope it would go away. Finally, Apple agreed that its screens were not properly coated and set up a $22.5 million fund to reimburse dissatisfied customers. The screen coating was improved to make the Nano more scratch resistant, and sales improved again. It's a lesson that Apple learned the hard way, and it now actively engages customers online and is much more responsive to any online complaints.

The importance and power of internet collaboration was demonstrated by workers at a Johnny Walker bottling plant in Kilmarnock, Scotland. Diageo is planning to close the plant with the loss of 700 jobs, and the workers lobbied the company to change its plans. When this was unsuccessful they enlisted the help of local politicians, and when they had little success they went to Parliament, and even gained the support of the Prime Minister, and fellow Scotsman, Gordon Brown. He also failed to persuade Diageo to keep the bottling plant open. So the workers turned to the most powerful lobbying tool: the internet. They hired Blue State Digital, which ran President Obama's highly successful online campaign. The company specializes in the development of online communities that can be mobilized as activists and lobbyists. The company is developing a campaign to put global pressure on Diageo through the use of the internet and its powerful collaborative and communal tools. This whole affair has been a public relations disaster for Diageo, and it may well now turn into an economic disaster if Blue State Digital can persuade people around the world to stop drinking Johnny Walker and other Diageo products.

Perhaps more effective collaboration between the company and its employees would have prevented this affair from becoming a global spectacle played out in the mass media and among the online community. Twenty-first-century businesses will need to respond to criticism very rapidly by either engaging in debate with their detractors, or making changes to their product. Failure to do so could result in irreversible damage to the reputation and sales of a company, and possibly even strike a fatal blow to its very existence. Managing online word of mouth will be the biggest issue for marketers in the twenty-first century. It will become a central pillar of every marketing plan, and essential to a company's welfare.

Net Promoter Score

The most successful single measure of customer satisfaction and predictor of growth is the net promoter score or NPS. It is a measure of both trust and satisfaction in a brand, service, or company. First developed by the management consultancy Bain & Co., the NPS was brought to prominence by Fred Reichheld in his book, *The Ultimate Question*. The NPS is based on a single question that every company should ask its customers, which is "How likely are you to recommend this [brand/company/service] to a friend?"

The response is scored on a scale of 1–10. Those who rate a company between 1 and 6 are classified as detractors. They are unlikely to recommend the company, and are more likely to say negative things about it than positive. Everyone in this group can damage a business when they "badmouth" the company to friends, colleagues, and complete strangers over the internet. People who rate the company 7–8 are viewed as passive or neutral. They are unlikely to be negative about the company, but aren't sufficiently impressed to go out of their way to praise it. If pushed, they will provide a balanced response, and be fair in their comments. Finally, promoters are those who rate the company in the top two boxes of 9 or 10. These are people who really like what they experienced and are very satisfied with what the company has to offer. They are highly likely not only to say nice things about a company, but to encourage other people to use it. They become *brand ambassadors*, who will positively influence the purchase decision of many others.

Empirical evidence has shown that companies which have a high NPS grow at a significantly faster rate than other companies. GE, P&G, Allianz, HSBC, and many other major corporations monitor NPS because they recognize the importance of positive word of mouth for a company, and the potential damage that can be caused by detractors.

Before the internet, word of mouth operated on a relatively small, local stage. Now it plays on a global arena in front of millions of people. Negative comments about a product in Canada will affect its sales in France. Complaints about a brand in Finland can change purchase decisions in Australia. Word of mouth must be managed and responded to, and the NPS needs to be measured. But most importantly, a process of collaboration needs to be established between a company and its customers, especially during the development of new products and services. If a company truly wants to meet the needs of customers it must collaborate with them in the product development process.

Horizontal Structure

Companies will also need to change from a hierarchical structure to a horizontal one, in which key decisions are made at the interface with the customer, not at the top of a bureaucracy. The most important people in twenty-first-century companies will be those who collaborate directly with their customers. These are the power and opportunity that collaboration offers. Companies that are online savvy and understand the power of collaboration will be in a better position not only to manage word of mouth comments about their brands, but also to solicit the assistance of their users in product design and functionality.

Usually it is those companies in the telecoms, computing, or online sector that have learned through painful experience how to manage web opinion and collaboration better. This is because their user groups are particularly vocal online and past damage, as happened to Apple with its iPod Nano, has taught companies the danger of adverse comment that isn't quickly dealt with. Usually online criticism relates to a product itself, but sometimes it can be related to the services or communications of a company.

Dell Computer, for example, was forced to respond to vociferous online criticism about its customer service. Very unhappy customers were beginning to damage Dell's business, not because of the products it sold, but the very poor general service levels. Michael Dell personally stepped in and created a website designed to specifically solicit customer ideas about how to improve Dell's service. The company's key executives also engaged in blogs and other dialogue with their users to understand complaints better and have them resolved. The result was that Dell collaborated with its customers to develop a better service capability and a more satisfactory business model. The company learned that it wasn't enough to simply sell products online; it needed to engage actively with its customers to find better ways to do business.

Perhaps the most bizarre example of online complaints changing a product occurred with the very business which is at the vanguard of networking and collaboration: Facebook. Facebook showed that even the most successful online networking companies can suffer the ire of their users if they make changes without consulting or collaborating with their customers. Most online and software sites issue beta versions of new products to gauge user reaction and find any flaws before launching the final version. However, Facebook, which is the ultimate collaborative tool, recently changed its format without first asking its 175 million users. It endured a torrent of fierce criticism, which gained enormous momentum and power in a just a few days. Facebook subsequently apologized and readjusted its site to meet the demands of its users. This incident showed that even the managers of the world's most successful networking website, which brilliantly tapped into people's desire for communication and community, didn't seem to understand the powerful dynamics of user collaboration to improve its product. The lesson is that customers will help create a website, a product, or a business if you let them.

If you create a framework, platform or basic model, users quickly let you know what interests them and what doesn't, what they like and what they don't want. The online and offline relationship with customers should be blended into one integrated whole. Companies that allow their customers to engage and share their passion for a product or service can gain considerable insight and benefit, which may lead to improvement and innovation. Using direct customer-generated information to modify a website, product, or service, can initiate a process of creation, continual improvement, user innovation, and almost infinite new business opportunities. It is for this reason that most companies in the twenty-first century will need to change to open-source, collaborative product development.

The shock and frustration that young people feel when they join a company and are asked to work using old Web 1.0 desktop applications provides an insight into the future of effective business practice in the twenty-first century. New employees now have a Web 2.0 mentality. These "digital natives" expect to be able to use new web-based tools to collaborate with colleagues, maintain real-time involvement in projects, and facilitate communication. Young employees assume that they can share and organize information, collaborate and connect with whomever is necessary to get the job done. If companies take this same mentality on board, and provide the tools to do the job, they will dramatically increase innovation, shorten development cycles, and engage all the brainpower within an organization. The larger and more geographically disparate a company, the more it is likely to benefit from collaboration.

However, using Enterprise 2.0 tools demands a flatter company structure, which is driven from the bottom up rather than top down. It needs to be agile and respond quickly to customer needs with a minimum of bureaucracy. It has to have open borders not silos. It has to be flexible and transparent. It needs to be organized for the twenty-first century, not just use its tools. The management consultants McKinsey found that the use of Web 2.0 tools by companies helped forge closer links with customers and suppliers, and engage better with employees. Companies that satisfactorily used the new collaborative tools saw them as boosting their competitive advantage, and McKinsey expects these businesses to become more aggressive in the marketplace versus slower rivals.

The pharmaceutical company Pfizer enjoyed great benefits when an employee downloaded some wiki software and created a "Pfizerpedia." He launched it within the company to serve as a scientific encyclopedia for worldwide employees. However, it rapidly took on a life of its own and "spread like a virus, filling voids, connecting dots, and attaining its own form—that of a high-level roadmap to research going on across the company, studded with hypertext links to detailed research," reported *Chemical & Engineering News*. A year after its launch, Pfizerpedia had 13,000 users worldwide, and has provided a platform for intelligence sharing, document collaboration, and joint developments. Even the CIA is using the wiki technology in its secure "Intellipedia," which contains all manner of information and discoveries to allow people to collaborate, compare information, and develop a 360-degree view of any topic. Collaborative techniques clearly pay dividends, and are being increasingly recognized as very valuable tools across diverse operations.

Customer Leadership

In his book *What Would Google Do?*, Jeff Jarvis explores how Google engages with its users and enlists their advice when it comes to new products and additional features and services. He proposes that companies should follow the same successful business model as Google and give up control of their product development to outside influences to reap the benefit of their input. Some of the most successful online businesses, including Google, are creating basic platforms but then allowing the users themselves to define how it should best work. As Jarvis says, "Many service providers could do well to make something useful then get out of the way."

By allowing users to participate in the creation of the design and functionality of a product, a company is completely in sync with its customers and their needs. The company's product becomes "co-owned" by the users, who have helped improve its design and operation to meet their needs precisely. This user-designed product then enjoys much greater loyalty and usage than other products that don't allow this collaboration and "open-sourcing" of ideas.

Throughout the twentieth century, politics and business have been hierarchical in nature and driven from the top down. Great business leaders have been eulogized as they conceived products and developed processes that delivered a plethora of new products to eager consumers. The status quo has been strengthened through MBA courses and business schools that have taught people how to be more effective managers in hierarchical corporations. How many books have we read on the secrets of effective management?

However, most business schools assume that companies in the twenty-first century will be organized in the same way as in the past. In this new century of collaboration, companies will increasingly be structured from the bottom up, not the top down. Businesses will need to reorganize themselves to create horizontal customer-led matrices, rather than vertical company-led structures. The most successful businesses will become horizontally innovative where direction comes straight from the "coal face," not vertically organized by a management structure far removed from customer relationships.

Effective businesses will need to collaborate closely with their customers, and the leaders of twenty-first century companies will engage with users to constantly refine products and services in real time. This century's successful companies will not have hierarchical management. They will have leaders who collaborate closely with their customers, and are supported by administrative and production services. Many companies pay lip-service to being "customer led," but they still predesign the products for customers. Merely checking on customer opinion about goods that have already been designed and manufactured is not being customer led. It is simply monitoring opinion in the context of existing products within a category. Really being customer led requires a process of collaborating openly with customers on the original design, function, and pricing, and then working to deliver to this need.

Therefore the key to future management will be to collaborate with customers in the design of exciting and original products and services. Innovative decisions relating to design, distribution, and services will all be made at the front line of the company, not at the "top of the company." In the future, businesses will need to clearly distinguish between customer-led management and company-led administration.

Perhaps the most hierarchical, old-style businesses are automobile manufacturers. Ask a car manufacturer if it seeks the opinion of its users before spending billions on its design and manufacture, and it will tell you that market research is undertaken at every stage of development. Unfortunately, the research is designed to reassure rather than originate. David Ogilvy had a wonderful comment about market research. He said that "most companies use research like a drunken man uses a lamppost: for support rather than illumination."

The car companies are no different. They provide a predetermined list of features and design options, and then ask consumers' opinions. The consumer isn't involved in the design itself or allowed to input ideas about features and functions, but simply to comment on what is put before him or her. Automobile manufacturers then conduct "positioning" research to establish a vehicle's relationship with other models in the category. Again, this is not being customer led, it is simply finding where a predetermined model design would fit into an existing product category. None of this is actually collaborative. It is simply asking opinions about a product that the manufacturer has already designed, not finding out what the consumers might have in mind and working with them to meet their specific needs. Companies need to truly collaborate with their customers at the early stages of product development, not restrict the dialogue simply to asking for feedback on something that has already been designed.

Interestingly, Ford is now designing vehicles with specific people in mind. Its market research develops a hypothetical user, and describes the lifestyle, attitudes, and values to its design team. Then it designs the vehicle to meet these needs. It's a step in the right direction, but it still shows a basic arrogance that the company knows best. Why doesn't it start by asking the prospective customers how *they* would design their own car? Why doesn't it design something *with* the consumers? Collaborate with the target consumers from the outset, and involve them in the design and specifications right through the entire development process.

Jeff Jarvis provocatively asks whether the Google business model could help the automobile industry. He urges car companies "to open up their design process and make it both transparent and collaborative." By being secretive, car companies have created a sameness of design and features, and a general category boredom. Perhaps the new generation of electric cars will take the opportunity to collaborate with potential customers and use their ideas to develop innovative vehicles and very different business models.

Futurist Stewart Brand famously said at a conference for computer hackers in 1984 that "information wants to be free." If we think of this in relation to collaborative business models and open-source business, the freedom of information can only help the rapid development of innovative, new products. The new ability to collaborate opens up powerful opportunities for individuals to involve themselves with the products and services that they use, and for companies to engage with their customers more closely in a mutually positive relationship. Collaborative and open-source product development has proven successful for many websites and service companies, but it offers huge possibilities for any kind of business in this interactive century.

The Power of Communities

This world of ours . . . must avoid becoming a community of dreadful fear and hate, and be, instead, a proud confederation of mutual trust and respect.
—Dwight D. Eisenhower, US president

Asking whether communities create collaboration, or the need to collaborate creates communities, is a chicken and egg question. The internet is enabling vast "virtual" communities, as social networks and special interest groups use the medium to create a much sharper sense of "we." However, there is also a significant increase in the number of "real" communities based around common values, beliefs, or behavior that collaborate in person. These communities may involve deeply held beliefs like environmentalism, or simply reflect common behavioral interests, such as education, health, or the arts.

Cults and collectives are other manifestations of communal behavior in which people who share the same religious or political belief band together to protect the interests of their community. Whatever the reason for the community, the members collaborate closely and are happy to proselytize their interests, beliefs, or values to add new adherents and enlarge their communal group. They are very inclusive and seek out people with common goals and similar perspectives. The ease with which new communities can be formed either online or offline, and the pace with which networking sites gather users, indicate that communities will be a powerful and influential force in the twenty-first century.

Community Self-Help Groups

Self-help groups will inevitably be a growing feature of twenty-first-century life. These groups involve action by committed people within a community who feel strongly about an issue, or want to add some support in areas where the state or the church are failing to do so. These communities are not usually organized online, and are very much focused on local needs. The activities of self-help groups can be as simple as helping someone who needs advice, or organizing activities for juveniles or older citizens.

In Singapore, there are groups devoted to encouraging racial harmony, and others to help students with their studies. Yet other groups help build cultural identity or work together to improve the local environment. Sometimes these communities attract government or charitable donations, but more often they are simply groups of people taking great pleasure from providing a helping hand in their community. Perhaps the strangest community that I heard about were the "guerilla gardeners" in London. This was group of keen gardeners who cringed at the neglect they saw of various public areas that could be beautified quite easily. They offered to cultivate the uncared-for areas and beautify them with flowers and plants. However, the local councils objected to the public doing the job of their employees, and the police worried that "gardeners" might vandalize public property. So a guerilla gardeners community was formed to plant flowers and plants secretly to beautify various public areas. They had to meet furtively late at night at an agreed rendezvous with their gardening tools and fresh plants. They then worked under cover of darkness to clear the land and plant new flowers and shrubs. When the gardening work was finished they would all smile and go home to bed satisfied that they had enjoyed themselves and helped the community. Sometimes they chose to improve the appearance of a traffic roundabout, and other times it would be the verge of a road, and occasionally a disused plot of land. They were all keen gardeners, so they were doing what they enjoyed most, while improving the environment for others. This, by the way, is selfish altruism at work!

The American version of this was Johnny "Appleseed" Chapman, who planted apple trees all over the Midwest on land that didn't belong to him. He was seen as a wonderful, altruistic man with an original community spirit. His mission wasn't entirely altruistic however, because he sold many of the saplings and fruit to make a comfortable living from it. Johnny would be very much at home in the Age of Selfish Altruism.

Giving Circles

There will also be greater participation in "giving circles," in which people with common beliefs, values, or ethical goals band together to fund a cause, charity, or worthy enterprise. Giving circles are usually concerned members of a local community who seek to make a specific impact in the area that concerns them. The individuals in the group pool their funds to donate to their specific cause, and the amount that each individual contributes can range from just a few dollars to many thousands. Members of a giving circle also usually commit their time and skills to the cause as well as providing funding, which further improves the social life of the community. Giving circles try to attract new members, so they spread their beliefs as well as provide charitable funding to their chosen cause.

Cooperatives and mutual aid societies have long existed to help local communities, and giving circles are really a modern, philanthropic extension of these organizations. They consist of like-minded individuals who band together to play a greater part in the community and contribute to its welfare and social life. Giving circles usually contribute to a wide range of local causes in their own community, from funding math education among inner city students to saving ancient woodlands. However, many giving circles are now developing a broader, international scope and are funding a wide range of activities from providing clean water access in Africa to gay and lesbian rights.

Crowdfunding

Crowdfunding has been powerfully enabled by the internet, and is very much associated with social networks and various online communities.

Crowdfunding doesn't often gather a permanent group of people together who are committed to a specific cause, as do giving circles. It usually attracts one-time contributions from a mass of online participants for a specific project. Most projects are commercial, and most contributions are small. However, the enormous size and scope of online networks mean that although the individual donation may be small, the volume is enormous, so large amounts of money can be garnered in a very short time.

As the name suggests, crowdfunding can be very much a function of crowd psychology, so the success of a project is often closely related to the timing and opportunism. Crowdfunding networks may gather to fund a specific project, then simply disappear when it is completed. They don't usually have the same communal binding as giving circles, which involve personal interaction between local individuals. Although many charitable contributions are made through crowdfunding, a sizable proportion of the donations seem to be directed to financing films, fashion, the arts, and online ventures. Many contributions can be "investments" rather than donations. However, the impact of crowdfunding is further evidence of the power of "community," which is being increased by the internet.

Cults

Although there is no data that I have found to confirm this assertion, anecdotal evidence leads me to believe that there are a growing number of cults across the world. Whether it is being a new age druid in the UK, or a Falun Gong adherent in China, or part of a Waco family in the US, more people seem to be drawn to cults and their communities. We read a lot about the Chinese government's opposition to Falun Gong. This cult teaches the importance of "truthfulness, compassion, and forbearance." It is not a religion, but its emphasis on morality and theological principles have generated both committed adherents and strong opposition from a slightly paranoid Chinese government.

Perhaps we all get somewhat paranoid about cults and the "threat" they pose, because by definition they are tight communities that exist within the overall population. Although most cults welcome new adherents, they do not welcome "outsiders," so their activities are unknown and apparently suspicious to anyone looking from the outside in. There have always been cults, and some have evolved into religions. In this new century of community activities, it seems highly likely that they will continue to thrive and prosper as common values bind people together.

The Family Unit

Of all communal activities, the strengthening of the family unit is the most important and powerful. The rise of "real values," combined with an impending pension crisis, plus the economic problems related to an aging population are creating closer family units. Partly this will happen because there will be no other viable option for many families. Either the parents need physical or economic assistance from their offspring, or new families find they need support from their parents. In other cases, families feel the emotional need to become closer and take care of each other. Whatever the reason, families are gathering together in closer units for mutual support and social satisfaction, and will continue to do so.

In large part, this movement toward closer family values will be driven by changing attitudes in the twenty-first century. There are strengthening beliefs that "friends and family" are what will matter most. There is a growing rejection of senseless luxury and acquisitions purchased simply to increase status.

A study among Singaporeans by one of the local banks, OCBC, asked people about their top 10 dreams and goals. The 2008 results listed the top three dreams as:

1. Seeing the world
2. Self-improvement
3. Making money.

The 2009 results were totally different:
1. Family and children
2. Settling down and starting a family
3. House and home.

This huge shift may have had something to do with the massive financial inducements that the Singapore government began to offer in 2008 to encourage married couples to have children and raise the birth rate. However, it is clear from this and other similar studies that the impact of the financial meltdown caused people to reflect on what was really important in life. As always in times of stress, the family, home, and security come out on top, as they will increasingly continue to do in this new moral century.

Evidence of stronger "family values" and closer family relationships is becoming much more apparent all around the world. For example, there has been strong growth of multigenerational households in the US. Either adult children and their families are moving into their parents' homes, or the parents are moving into their children's households. The number of homes in the US containing both a parent and their adult children grew 67 percent between 2000 and 2008.

Variety Magazine recently stated "Entertainment worldwide is returning to 'back to basics' and wholesome fare for the whole family." Dramas with feel-good and traditional themes are replacing shows with cutthroat competition such as *The Apprentice*. Programming that appeals to the whole family, not just a specific segment, will attract greater audiences as family units draw closer together. The return of all-family viewing may well accelerate the trend toward a large fixed screen for communal viewing at home and a small, mobile, personal screen for each individual.

British Sky Broadcasting predicted that entertainment will increasingly be sought in the home. "The strength of the home" in the context of economic problems delivered their fastest subscriber increase for years in 2008. However, the CEO predicted that "this is the start of a longer-term trend." The family home will be more of a "castle" in the future, not primarily an investment vehicle as it has been for the past few decades. The home will be a point of stability and comfort. A house will be a place where DIY is undertaken to improve lifestyle, not necessarily the value of the property. A base for taking care of the family as well as oneself will be a key feature of the new Age of Selfish Altruism. This change in perspective about a home, from investment to family castle, means that buyers will take a longer-term perspective with more practical values.

Better Homes & Gardens magazine conducted a survey among new home buyers in the US to discover what key factors would affect their choice of property. The magazine discovered six top priorities:

- family gathering areas
- energy efficiency
- no-space-wasted design
- natural light
- ample storage space
- of course, an affordable price.

The magazine's editor-in-chief, Gayle Butler, said, "Following an era of 'supersizing' our lifestyles and our homes, consumers are coming back down to earth with a new frame of mind." An astounding 63 percent of respondents said that they consider comfortable family gathering areas a top priority. "We're seeing more interest in Wii-sized spaces, 'media-centric' family rooms that can accommodate a variety of activities—from board games to videogames, Wii dance and fitness systems," Butler went on to say.

The same family-focused perspective carried through to the kitchen and dining areas, where the majority of respondents said they would prefer to have a combined kitchen, family room and everyday eating area.

Finally, environmentally friendly elements were a top priority for new-home buyers with 90 percent planning to have energy-efficient heating and cooling systems, and a really surprising 31 percent who intend to have geothermal heat. Again we see the combination of increasing environmental concerns, new values, and the influence of closer, communal family ties being reflected in lifestyle decisions. All the big trends of the twenty-first century are coming together in the home.

Feeding the Mind as Well as the Body

Voyages of self-discovery and opportunities for self-development will be increasingly important activities. Self-discovery may come through physical or "virtual" relationships and understanding, and will become increasingly important as people re-evaluate what is important in their lives in the Age of Selfish Altruism. Discovering the "real me" and finding the "secret to true happiness" will become increasingly important, especially as we age. People in the twenty-first century will spend more years at employed work than humans have ever undertaken in the past. Long, extended working years will partly be necessary either because government pensions will demand later retirement, or individuals need to accumulate more money to fund their retirement.

However, staying at work may also be a lifestyle choice to stave off boredom in later life. Sometimes, continued employment will be due to both economic necessity and social choice. These factors will likely result in a lot more part-time employment. People will enjoy a couple of days a week to provide interest and social activity, with the added bonus of some extra cash.

More people will find "late-stage careers" or start their own business using networking sites such as LinkedIn and Xing to generate contacts and create opportunity. This will all satisfy the desire to create communities and stay physically and mentally active. Even with long extended working years, it is likely that most people will look forward to a retirement period of 20 years or more. This will result in an increasing demand for "extracurricular" activities. Hobbies and mind-broadening activities will become much more important in people's minds. Developing a parallel life to what is often the drudgery of work will become a primary mission.

Among aging consumers, there will be an added zeal to pursue adult education and second life interests. The need to feed and exercise the brain as well as the body will become even more important. Late degrees that "I've always wanted to take," or interests that grew out of, or into, full-time hobbies will be a feature of communal life in this century. To be the best I can be will again become a mantra, but it will be measured by self-worth and happiness, not economic success.

Socially Active, Healthy Lifestyles

Maintaining a socially active, healthy lifestyle will also be a major goal of both individuals and government in the twenty-first century, and will involve entire communities. From a governmental perspective, an aging and increasingly unfit population will put enormous strain on health and care services. So encouraging their population to remain active and healthy will be a major goal of government. Every effort will be made to reduce obesity, catch coronary problems early, and identify cancer or other serious illnesses at an early stage. Prevention of illness and encouragement of wellness activities will be key focuses of the health services. Personal genome data can help identify and manage or nullify potential illnesses at an early stage in life. Continuous monitoring of vital health statistics will enable faster diagnosis and corrective or preventive action.

As we will discuss later, the requirement to maintain good health will become a central government policy and it will demand new responsibilities to be shared among many constituencies, not least of which will be the individuals themselves. This will be something that people will want and appreciate, rather than being an imposition. Individuals will share the desire to maintain wellbeing and extend their active lives to create a balanced lifestyle: the ability to keep working longer while maintaining a social and communal focus. There will be an increasing demand for keep-fit activities that, for older people especially, are not too physically punishing and have an element of social interaction.

The social aspect has always been important in many sports, but aging and more communal lifestyles will strengthen this aspect of well-being activities. Although traditional social activities such as team sports, golf, sailing, and cycling, with their associated clubs, will enjoy stronger support, other activities may even bring a more spiritual satisfaction such as tai chi, qigong, and yoga. Health clubs and sports activities can maintain fitness and deliver social, community opportunities that many people are searching for. So health clubs will become mandatory for any apartment building, community centers, and office buildings.

The importance of finding social activities to maintain wellbeing becomes greater with age, as a person passes through the lifestages that naturally provide community activity such as school, job, and even family. Staying active becomes very important to everyone who wants to maintain a social life.

Maintaining health and wellbeing will also mean a greater emphasis on healthy eating with a nutritional focus. Fighting flab is always difficult, and becomes a lot harder with age. Maintaining a steady weight is a function of exercise as well as caloric intake. So aging populations will turn to low-calorie drinks and focus on more nutritional, healthy eating to maintain a satisfactory weight and wellbeing. "My body is a temple" is unlikely to be a widespread mantra, but people will do what they can to stay in good health. Interest in colonic irrigation, detoxing, and other "body-cleansing" activities and products may well become more popular as "secrets to a longer, healthier life." Marketers will find that the sale of junk food will become more difficult. As governments force more precise caloric and dietary information to be clearly printed on every product sold, consumers may well be shocked as they understand the implication of what they are eating. So food providers will need to increasingly provide reassurance about the provenance and nutritional benefits of their products. At the very least, consumers will need to know that they are doing no harm to either the environment or the ecology, and that they are consuming something from a sustainable product source.

The Law of Happiness

The power and importance of social and communal values is best summed up by the Law of Happiness. I'm not really a great proponent of the "make love not war" and "if you love someone, set them free" school of popular aphorisms. Most of the *Desiderata* stuff of my youth I cast aside, and a lot of the "Secret of Happiness" guff that is sent to me I delete in a nanosecond. However, I must say that the Law of Happiness fits very well into the community values that are strengthening as we enter the Age of Selfish Altruism. So here it is:

The Law of Happiness: if you want to stay happy then you have to keep others happy.

Every individual is surrounded by five circles of people:

- *The first or the innermost circle* consists of people you come into contact with the most, daily or very frequently. Examples are your wife or husband and co-workers.

- *The second circle* that surrounds the first are the people you meet once or twice a week and not as frequently as in the first circle. Examples are friends you meet, people you visit, or fellows in the gym or a class that you are taking.

- *The third circle* surrounds the second and consists of individuals you meet once or twice a year or perhaps less often. You know all these people, but you just don't have the time or opportunity to see them more often. Examples are distant relatives and old friends.

- *The fourth circle* consists of people you don't know but can meet at any time. Examples are the attendant at a grocery store, someone you say good morning to in the elevator, or a person you nod to on the train home every evening.

- *The fifth circle* comprises people you don't know or haven't met, but these people know you. Examples are of fans of rock stars, famous businesspeople, or authors.

Your personal happiness depends on how happy the individuals are with you, in all five circles. To achieve absolute happiness all the people in all these five circles should be happy with you. After first reading this Law of Happiness, I regretted being so rude to my ex-wives (only joking!), being short tempered with that shop assistant yesterday, and sending insulting notes to the management of Newcastle United Football Club. I also wished I'd stayed closer to old friends and been nicer to my work colleagues. But all is not lost! Happiness is still within reach for me thanks to social networks, improved telecommunications, and a gradual improvement in my interpersonal skills as age slowly tempers my normally sarcastic nature. I must seize the opportunity that the big trends of collaboration and community are providing me with, and strive harder for happiness.

The Power of Consensus

9

In this context, social consensus, and institutions that embody this consensus, must be made effective in order for democratization not to be abused.

—Rece Tayyip Erdogan,
Turkish prime minister

Consensus building may become much easier to achieve because ease of collaboration and greater community spirit allow people to join forces on many issues. The internet provides an often impersonal but highly effective forum for public debate. The speed of exchange, easy access, and equality of voice allow active and effective discussion. Consensus building has become a lot faster and the number of people who are involved can quickly build into the millions. The result is that great pressure can be exerted on companies or governments to deliver change and take action.

In the same way that word of mouth can damage a brand or company, it can just as easily affect a government or individual politician. Public servants must therefore become much more conscious of the collaborative effects of networking and community groups to build a consensus on any issue. Lobbying by various community groups will become much more aggressive and new social issues will gain traction at an almost unbelievable speed. In the past, governments conceived and established policies based on their political party's tenets, and then "sold" their ideals to the voters.

In the future, voters will set the agenda, and governments will need to respond, regardless of their party or underlying beliefs. Governments will increasingly be driven to create new policies and legislation by direct popular pressure of newly "enfranchised" online social communities. The powerful social networking of the internet will allow citizens to collaborate and then address politicians in a much more direct way than was ever realistically possible in the past. No government will survive if it doesn't listen to the groundswell of opinion on the internet, and make it part of its political agenda. Collaboration, community, and consensus will be central to government policy and action.

I recently talked to some politicians who were keen to learn how to "use the internet" to help them with an upcoming election. They credited the internet for both Obama's win and the success of other politicians in a range of different countries. The power of online communication with voters has not been lost on any politician, whether in America or Malaysia, India or Spain. Unfortunately, they had difficulty understanding that it wasn't the medium itself that won those elections, it was the collaboration and consensus that it enabled. The internet is a superb medium for *interactive communication*, which makes possible a sense of community and the ability to achieve consensus of opinion through active collaboration.

The internet itself wasn't any more responsible for an election win than television was in the past. Or radio before that. Of course every new medium creates fresh opportunities and unforeseen problems. Radio made oral communications and a trustworthy tone of voice more important. Television made facial appearance and charisma much more critical. Television was famously credited with causing the loss of a US presidential election by a perspiring Richard Nixon, who had refused TV makeup, to John Kennedy who appeared younger, more dynamic—and without sweat on his forehead.

The internet offers a new medium for collaboration and consensus building, not just one-way communication as radio and TV and print media did in the past. It is the innovation that a new medium allows that helps win elections, not just the medium itself. Marshall McLuhan famously stated that the medium is the message, meaning that the internet itself may actually affect the process of thought. It is certainly true that the internet lends itself to politics by providing a platform that encourages the fast pace and "soundbite" communication of Twitter and various internet-based blogs. But ultimately it is the effectiveness of the interactive communication that is critical. Every new medium provides the platform to shape the communication of ideas and perspectives to the electorate.

The New Twenty-First-Century Morality

10

Morality, like art, means drawing a line someplace.

—Oscar Wilde

The big trends of environmentalism, "post-consumerism," and demographic change are already affecting this century and their effects are becoming more apparent globally. These major trends are all contributing to a "new morality," which will become increasingly influential and powerful as it moves up the bell curve of mainstream acceptance.

"Consumers are now becoming more eager to demonstrate conspicuous virtue rather than conspicuous consumption," according to JWT. "Yesterday's rewards are today's guilty pleasures." With guilt being the operative word! The growing concern and consensus about the need for global action to halt climate change and prevent further ecological damage is playing a key role in creating this new morality. Schools are teaching young children how to protect the environment and all the living creatures in it, but with a fervor that would have been seen as "weirdly green" or "eco crazy" just a generation ago.

The increasing number of older people who feel some guilt at the damage they have inadvertently caused during their time on the planet has generated powerful moral support for action to prevent further environmental deterioration and repair the world for future generations. The growth of online social networking has created a new feeling of "global empowerment." Netizens have found that there are millions of others with similar beliefs and interests and values who come from disparate backgrounds and geographies.

These interests and values are manifesting themselves through various communal and social activities, which are creating broad consensual opinions with strong moral underpinnings. No longer are we bound by geography or language, race or religion. We have learned to communicate and share our feelings, interests, and beliefs with a wide global community. And we're finding that millions of others share our sentiments and morality. This "new morality" will affect attitudes, behavior and product development over the course of the twenty-first century. We are already seeing a huge shift toward "green consumerism" and ethical buying standards.

The Futures Company conducted a recent study to gauge changes of attitude and awareness of environmental issues in the UK, and found that there had been significant recent increases. The company concluded that: "If the aspiration toward an ethical and sustainable life was once regarded as the preserve of fringe groups, 'sustainability' has now entered mainstream discourse. There is a momentum to this rising tide of ethical and environmental conscience." The Futures Company found for example that 86 percent of Britons wanted reduced packaging on the products they bought, and 82 percent felt it was important to buy local goods from nearby shops. These are extremely high percentages in a diverse population. It was also very clear from the study that people had a strong desire to live more ethically and wanted to buy more ethically produced goods. A significant proportion of people felt guilty about not living as ethically as they would like to, which showed in a growing level of guilt about things such as taking short-haul flights, driving their car when they should take public transport, and strong support for banning four-wheel-drive vehicles from urban areas.

The research did find a difference between aspiration and action. People wanted to live an ethically stronger life, but were not prepared to inconvenience themselves greatly to achieve this goal. Many other studies have found similar results, which have been used to disparage consumer commitment to ethical and environmentally friendly products. It has been argued that although people express a desire to live more ethically, they actually take little action to support their views. Personal sacrifice is always hard to make, especially if it involves inconvenience or cost. That is just normal, sensible human behavior. However, if the latent *desire* is there, governments will need to respond, and manufacturers have a terrific opportunity to satisfy that need. Consumers want ethical and environmentally safe products, and study after study has shown that most people would happily pay a premium to buy these goods. So failing to cater to such a strong trend is unforgivable for the corporate world.

Ethical Consumption

As the desire for higher ethical standards becomes ever stronger, it is clear that consumers seize on every convenient opportunity to achieve the moral satisfaction of doing something to achieve their goals. Any chance to change to an ethical product without any great cost or inconvenience is being taken by consumers. It is up to manufacturers to provide the opportunity for customers to feel morally safe about the purchases they make, and allow them to feel warm and satisfied about what they are buying. The Futures Company found that although people very much want to live more ethically, they do not want to make all the personal sacrifices necessary *unless everyone else does*. So people expect government to take the lead on environmental issues, which will very much be a feature of the twenty-first century. There will be a great deal of new legislation and aggressive policing of mandates that satisfy the consumer demand for environmental responsibility.

This same study also indicated a much "harder line" toward irresponsible and unethical behavior: 60 percent of respondents felt that people who fail to recycle should be punished. They also believe that companies that act unethically should be "heavily penalized." This hardening of attitudes toward ethical behavior is now very much part of mainstream thought. It is beginning to affect what people buy, how they behave, and what government policies they demand.

Another WPP Group company, TNS, carried out a global survey covering more than 13,000 people in 17 countries to evaluate green consciousness. TNS found that 40 percent of people globally say they have already changed their behavior to benefit the environment, and more than half claim that they would pay more for environmentally friendly products. So whether the respondents in this study lived in Argentina or Hong Kong, Spain or Korea, the US or Russia, they are all developing similar ethical and environmental standards. Interestingly, this TNS research and several other studies indicate that environmental awareness seems to be very high in developing countries. For example, the number of people who claim to have recently changed their behavior "a great deal" or "a good amount" is highest in Mexico (74 percent), Thailand (68 percent), Argentina (67 percent), and Brazil (65 percent). This compares with the much lower numbers in the US (36 percent), Japan (34 percent), and Germany (28 percent). The reason could be that the more-developed countries have already adopted a more ethical and environmentally friendly lifestyle, and new behaviors are only progressing in smaller increments. However, as I note later, developing countries have suffered some scandalous environmental and toxic product problems recently, so "green consciousness" is very high.

This change in consumer attitudes and behavior is slowly being recognized by retailers and manufacturers. Many supermarkets are now engaging in "choice editing," which is the removal of products from their shelves that are seen as unethical or environmentally unfriendly. The "unsafe" products are being replaced by goods that meet the ethical standards of their shoppers. The customers are happier because the retailer makes it easier for them to live in the morally and ethically sound manner to which they aspire. Manufacturers are also finding that ethical and environment reassurance on their packaging is becoming essential communication to both consumers and retailers.

It is quite clear that the emerging "new morality" has been created and nurtured by growing environmental and product concerns, but it has also sparked a new sense of ethics that covers much broader areas than climate change and pollution. As the Futures Company and TNS studies show, there is now a strong "moral outrage" about people and companies that act unethically. Because the *desire* to act ethically is so strong among consumers, they clearly feel a sense of guilt and frustration that they are not able to live in the moral way they aspire to. This frustration shows itself in the hardening attitudes toward unethical people and companies, and will increasingly force government into taking severe action.

Morality will be a common theme running through every aspect of life in this century. Sometimes moral issues will be quite blatant and open. Abortion, for example, creates great passion on both sides of the debate between pro-lifers and those concerned about the mental and social implications of unwanted pregnancy. The ongoing debate about stem cell research is an example of a potentially significant health benefit for all humans being passionately opposed by many people, including the Pope. It is the source of the cellular material which is creating a moral dilemma for many people, especially when cells are taken from human embryos. This and many other moral debates will become far more common and intense in the course of this century.

Ethical Science

Biotechnology, genetics, and nanotechnology will probably be three of the most important areas for research in the twenty-first century, and the basis for giant new companies. The most influential global corporations of the twentieth century, such as GM, Kodak, or Coca-Cola, will likely be replaced by biotechnology companies in the twenty-first century. These giant new corporations will span the globe and become immensely powerful. Pharmaceutical companies today, although large and influential, do not have the enormous sociopolitical power of a GM in its heyday. The new biotech companies of the twenty-first century will have the secret to life itself, and will become behemoths that dictate terms to governments and the populace alike.

These new biotech giants will not only provide "new-generation" medicines, but also replacement organs, bone and tissue-growth technology, genetic adaptation processes, and cloning to order. These mind-blowing innovations are very, very scary. Biotech corporations will be able to create a Frankenstein's monster, or any other type of creature or living organism. Who will control them and how far should they be allowed to go? This will be one of the key ethical debates that will dominate the new morality of the twenty-first century. The ethical line needs to be drawn between advances that can provide cures for human diseases, and the creation of new human parts or humans themselves.

Hardly a day goes by now without news reports saying "Science unlocks the secret of . . . " or "Breakthrough in the fight against . . . " Extraordinary progress is being made in all kinds of scientific arenas, especially in the area of "genomics," where genetic codes are broken and solutions to health problems discovered. As scientific discovery progresses, the complexity and implications of medical breakthroughs will become harder to understand, and the moral issues more difficult to resolve. Technology for example will soon give us the ability to create human life, but is it morally correct to do so?

Dolly the sheep ushered in a new world of cloning. Already many different species of mammals are being cloned. But is it right to do so, and at what point should we draw the moral line? When will the first human be cloned? When it eventually does happen, will the excuse be "because the same DNA is needed to save a sibling" or some other "moral" reason? Or will it be because a nation decides that its population decline needs to be reversed and sees no harm in cloning all of its inhabitants?

The first cloned human will cause us all to think very carefully about the implications of "playing God," and create a serious moral dilemma, whatever its stated reason.

Humans are already providing a single egg that can be fertilized by unknown sperm, and then raised in a test tube and a surrogate mother. And now this surrogacy can be taken further, because scientists at Newcastle University have discovered how to create sperm itself. The law presently forbids the use of artificial sperm with humans, but we all must fear that this resolve may be gradually eroded as science drives ever forward. Is all this morally correct, and where will it lead?

At what point in time will some horrible error occur and we bring to life a mythological half-man, half-beast? An indication of just how close we are to human creation was reported in the *Wall Street Journal* of July 27, 2009, headlined "New Chinese research raises ethical issues." It reported that Chinese scientists had "reprogrammed" cells from the skin of a mouse and converted them back to an embryonic state. These "reprogrammed" cells were used to create a live baby mouse offspring. Eeek! Not because they created a mouse, but "eek!" because of the implications.

Cells from a human could simply be taken from his or her skin, reprogrammed and injected into an embryo to create a human "chimera": a child who shares genes from two people but isn't the result of natural reproduction. The cells could be also be reprogrammed to produce specific genetic traits in this chimera. How are we going to feel about a new breed of chimeras with specific traits? The *WSJ* calls this development an "ethical challenge," and it is one we will all have to face in the very near future.

Drawing the line between medical advances and growing live creatures with specialist functions will be a very important ethical decision in the twenty-first century. Many countries already offer DNA profiling of a child to find latent or potential talents. The DNA is analyzed to find whether the child has a propensity that can be groomed, and thus make them a leader in that field of activity when they grow older. Families are using this DNA guidance to place children into certain sports activities, or to focus their education toward specific areas of "talent."

I really worry that allowing parents to obsess about making their child a "star" will encourage more streaming and specialization at a young age. This is likely to result in a lot more spoiled brats, who may be talented but fail to develop social skills necessary for an enjoyable, engaging life.

Robotics

Robotics will also be another enormous and influential industry in the twenty-first century. Technological innovation is again providing the means to create robots with extraordinary capabilities. We marvel at the abilities of mechanical robot cleaners, waiters, and attendants to undertake various tasks and perform extraordinary functions. Climbing stairs or picking up and placing an object, and many other mechanical tasks, cause us to applaud the new generation of robots now emerging in Japan. Robots are now acting as chefs in noodle shops, cleaners in offices as well as workers in factories. However, the big issue will arise when robots either look like humans, or are given the ability to think like a human.

It is almost inevitable that we will give anthropomorphic values to robots and attribute human values and characteristics to them. Just as we do to dogs and cats and other nonhuman "friends." We will name them and treat them as family members. Will you give your robot a human name, or a technical name, or just his or her model number? I think that most of us will give our robot a name as we imbue it with human values. It is possible that a robot will be viewed in the same way as a car, but I doubt that we'll treat a helper that lives in our home the same way that we do an inanimate car that sits idly in the garage.

Brand names will be handy references and even a source of prestige, rather like having a Porsche or a Mercedes: "Wow, you've got a new Panasonic Handyclean Auto 22! She must have cost a fortune. Maybe you can bring it over to my house and we could give her a test run?" No matter what the bragging rights may be outside the house, I am certain that we will give every robot in our home a "personal" name. They may even be able to be programmed to respond to their name: "Jeeves, may I have a gin and tonic please?"

It's easy to be humorous about robots and their human-serving abilities, but there is a very serious side to robotic innovation. *The challenge will be to ensure that robots do not become indistinguishable from humans!* I know it sounds ridiculous at this point, but we may have great difficulty physically distinguishing between humans and robots in the future. *Terminator* and many other sci-fi movies have long predicted robots or "humanoids" that have the appearance of humans, but contain mechanical interiors. These creatures may not only look and act like humans, but could eventually have an intellect that allows free thought. This is not as farfetched as it sounds. Already advances in biotechnology and genetics will allow us to grow skin cell by cell. This skin covering would help make robots look like humans. We will soon be able to create or clone brains, and create human organs.

I don't believe that anything will stop robotic innovation, and any opportunity to make robots more human in their functions and abilities will be seized upon with alacrity. Having a robotic servant in the home to take care of all the cleaning, washing, and household chores would be wonderful, particularly as the population ages and more people live alone. Rapidly aging societies will find robots essential, cost-efficient helpers, when caring for the elderly.

Other than occasional servicing they won't cost a cent to employ, so I can't think of any *practical* reason to stop the development of robots. However, if we have *moral* doubts, where do we draw the line? It's a decision that will likely go on being deferred until a robot runs amok and maliciously kills someone in a fit of rage. Then a line will be drawn. Until then, we will push forward with every innovation available to create the most "human," responsive robots with a broad range of capabilities.

Robots will be ecologically safe and they will not consume food or use much of the Earth's materials. They can be recycled. They will be invaluable assistants for older people. They will be the workers a country needs if depopulation occurs. They will be easy to communicate with, and provide comfort, convenience, and support to their owners.

The Future Moral Consensus

Morality is herd instinct in the individual.
—Friedrich Nietzsche

Big moral debates will be a feature of the twenty-first century. Whether about bio-technology, or genetic engineering, or robotics, the issues will become more complex, and opinion will likely be swayed by communal emotion, rather than pure logic. Our ethics and morality will increasingly be steered by new consensus-driven networks and organizations, which will exert enormous pressure on governments and public opinion by being able to deliver tens of millions of active supporters. Few politicians, or even individuals, will oppose the majority view because there will be a moral and social pact driven by "the common good."

This consensus will increasingly be tested by ever more complex moral issues, which will create tensions among church, state, science, business, and the general population. We saw similar ethical debates raging in the nineteenth century over slavery, popular emancipation, human rights, and the legitimacy of aggressive religious conversion. Darwin's "survival of the fittest" theories of natural selection created an enormous moral debate, which continues to this day. Churchgoers in the nineteenth century formed lobby groups to promote a cause, and new organizations such as the Salvation Army sprang up to provide support to the underprivileged. Propagandists such as author Charles Dickens forced readers to consider the unfairness that existed in society. Lobby groups were powerful mobilizers in the nineteenth century and continued to be in the twentieth century as female emancipation and alcohol-related issues brought thousands of people onto the streets to change opinions and laws. The antiwar protests of the 1930s and 1960s, and the Campaign for Nuclear Disarmament were all based on deep moral convictions.

The twenty-first century will continue to see mass protests over moral issues, but the form of protest and the sheer numbers involved will be staggering. The internet enables global networks to mobilize millions of people in support of a cause. There may sometimes be fewer people marching on the streets, but there will be far greater numbers spreading the word and delivering support online. Instead of waving banners, they will bombard their target audiences with aggressive emails and text messages. Online social networking sites are increasingly being used as political tools. Facebook is now far more than a social network, and who would ever have imagined Twitter could be a revolutionary tool to threaten a government, as recently happened in Iran?

All sorts of religious and community-based groups can now gather new adherents and mobilize massive numbers of people with relative ease if their moral cause is righteous. An example of this pressure arose in New Zealand, where users of social networking sites set up "Boycott Cadbury" groups to persuade people not to buy the company's products because it had added palm oil to its chocolate. Auckland Zoo removed all Cadbury's products from its shops and restaurants, and stated its concern about the damage that palm oil plantations do to the rainforests. The "Boycott Cadbury" groups then developed a petition to urge Parliament to warn consumers about the dangers of palm oil production. This demonstrates the extraordinary mobilization of opinion that can be achieved in a short space of time over a tiny incident where a trusted company simply changes from one type of oil to another.

Over the past few decades we have seen many large corporations attacked over ethical issues, and lobbying groups have been extremely effective even before the power of the internet emerged. Nestlé and Exxon continue to be affected by active and aggressive lobbying that attacks the "immorality" of both companies. Its detractors claim that *Exxon Valdez* was not simply an environmental disaster, but dramatic evidence of an avaricious corporation whose ethics and work practices have no regard for the planet or its ecology. Nestlé is accused of preventing the healthy, natural development of babies in underdeveloped countries by bribing mothers to use their milk powder rather than breastfeeding. These campaigns have been a thorn in the side of both companies for more than three decades, and still they linger on after becoming embedded in the minds of certain generations.

Procter & Gamble endured aggressive criticism by church groups who claimed that their trademark was a sign of the devil. P&G as the great Satan seems laughable to most people (except Unilever employees), but it did generate significant problems for the company in the US.

Ethical Criticism

Most multinational corporations have endured some sort of ethical protests, usually relating to unfair working conditions, in which workers or their rights have been abused, or environmental damage that their products are said to have caused. A whole new range of ethical issues are emerging to chivvy corporations to change their business practices. As ethical standards and beliefs broaden in their scope, we can expect more consumer backlashes over existing and new issues. So business needs to anticipate that the frequency and volume of ethical and moral criticism will increase, with lobbying groups more effectively using new as well as traditional media.

Greenfluencers

Porter Novelli identified a small but powerful group of consumers that they called "greenfluencers." They only account for about 4 percent of American consumers, but seem to be driving trends and influencing other shoppers. These "greenfluencers" aren't advocates who are trying to shape everyone's buying agenda; they are simply a diverse group of younger people who have strong opinions about social and political issues. Greenfluencers were "discovered" in a broad study by Porter Novelli in which consumers were labeled according to their behavior on seven different product or service criteria. These criteria ranged from buying energy-efficient appliances to refusing to buy from companies with a poor environmental record. The overall study revealed that only 16 percent of Americans had little or no concern for the environment, but the other 84 percent had different levels of "greenness," ranging from concerned "light green" to the highly committed "dark green." A small group of just 4 percent of Americans fell into the category between medium and dark green, but they appeared to be highly influential because others sought their opinions. This small but influential group was called "greenfluencers." Environmental decisions can often be confusing or difficult, and that is why many people ask the opinions of others. "Greenfluencers" have a great deal of environmental knowledge, and a clear rationale for their behavior, so this is why their opinion is valued and sought after. Although only representing a small proportion of American shoppers, they wield an influence which is way larger.

A WPP study across seven major countries asked how important it was for companies to be "green." At least 77 percent of respondents in every country said that greenness is important or very important. Surprisingly, the highest levels of agreement were found in India and China, where consumers said that corporate reputation and trustworthiness are very important purchase considerations. A staggering 98 percent of Indians, 97 percent of Chinese, and 93 percent of Brazilians felt strongly that companies should be "green." There was general agreement that the most environmentally important thing that a company could do was to reduce the amount of toxic and other dangerous substances in its products and processes. Environmental concerns in this and other studies consistently show China, India, and Brazil to be the countries most concerned about environmental issues, corporate ethics, and product safety. The reason is almost certainly because of past and current environmental damage that these countries have suffered.

The Great Stink and the Great Smog raised British sensibilities to environmental issues, and toxic waste, nuclear scares, and automobile fumes did the same in America. Now the big developing economies are facing similar types of issues or specific environmental or product problems that have raised environmental awareness and corporate concern. The environment has always taken a back seat to the need for economic growth when a country undergoes primary industrial development. As governments try to pull millions of their people out of poverty through rapid economic development, slowing that rate of growth by imposing strict environmental standards is rarely a policy that is willingly adopted. As a result, it is only when environmental catastrophes occur that both the government and the population realize that they should not be looking at growth versus environment. The two have to go hand in hand.

Environmental Protest

Economic growth doesn't automatically mean improvement in the quality of life. Environmental consciousness has become very top of mind in China after problems with tainted milk powder and other food contamination, dangerous lead poisoning, Beijing Olympic air pollution, water and river contamination, and a multitude of land development issues. People in China are becoming increasingly outraged about the never-ending environmental scandals, and are asking why the government isn't acting to *prevent* the problems, not simply reacting after the event.

In Brazil, the city of Cubatoa and its local area became known as the "valley of death." This industrial centre suffered hundreds of deaths from pipeline leakage explosions, appalling air pollution and respiratory problems, high levels of skin cancer and leukemia, and heavy metal pollution of the earth. The high profile of the Cubatoa problem, plus urban pollution, and of course the ongoing Amazon rainforest destruction have made environmental issues a significant concern in Brazil. India's environmental problems go all the way back to the Bhopal gas poisonings of 1984, which was probably the world's worst single-event environmental disaster with a death toll in excess of 20,000 people. The recent strong economic growth is now creating all the same environmental issues in Indian cities that China and Brazil have already suffered. In addition, climatic change is creating problems in rural areas. Much of northwest India has suffered from drought and severe water shortage. Excessive pumping and poor rainfalls will soon result in an agricultural irrigation and consumer household crisis in many parts of India as the water tables decline. It is no wonder then that the populations of these huge developing countries are very concerned about both the overall environment and specifically the safety of products they consume.

However, if there is a silver lining in this situation, it is that environmental concern can also be a huge marketing opportunity (sorry to be so crassly commercial, but there is an opportunity that could benefit business *and* consumers *and* the environment). The WPP "green" study showed that consumers in every country assumed that green products would cost more than nongreen goods. Nevertheless, most consumers in all countries said they were prepared to spend more on green products, most notably 73 percent of Chinese and Brazilians, and 78 percent of Indians. The percentage of respondents who indicated a willingness to spend *30 percent or more* on green products ranged from only 8 percent of people in the UK to 38 percent in Brazil. It seems clear from these figures that consumers in developing countries have a significant environmental concern, and an even greater willingness to take action. This indicates both stronger political will for environmental improvement, and a far greater economic propensity to buy "green" products. The biggest issue for manufacturers seems to be actually meeting consumer demand.

The research showed considerable frustration among consumers everywhere, but particularly in the big developing nations, about the difficulty in finding environmentally safe products. The biggest complaints were that the packaging and labeling is unclear, or environmental and ethical reassurances completely lacking. Consumers also wanted biodegradable or recyclable packaging. So there is a clear and unequivocal consumer demand for environmental and ethical reassurance that most manufacturers and retailers are completely missing. One of the study's sponsors in India articulated this problem and opportunity, "Indian consumers are concerned about the environment and would love to spend more on green products, but they don't know how to because of limited choice, limited distribution and limited labeling. This implies a huge latent opportunity for brands to tap into the power of green and create greater relevance for consumers."

Awareness of ethical issues can be generated globally with lightning speed. The broad reach of global television news channels and the size and loyalty of communal and networking sites offered by the internet, can communicate with tens of millions of people in seconds. Any subsequent pressure by a lobbying group can be intense because it mobilizes a very large number of people who try to quickly effect change. Greenpeace is probably the best example of a powerful lobby group that garners publicity through spectacular stunts, and can apply direct pressure on governments and corporations. Pressure by Greenpeace is forcing Unilever to obtain all the palm oil it uses in its products from sustainable sources: a move that the eco-warrior Prince Charles warmly praised. Hewlett-Packard recently "enjoyed" Greenpeace activists climbing to the top of its HQ with a banner reminding it of its 2007 commitment to remove toxic chemicals from its products. The French and Japanese governments have been consistently pressured by Greenpeace over nuclear tests and whaling; and the Brazilian and Indonesian governments are constantly hounded to do more to prevent the destruction of their rainforests.

This sort of aggressive "ethical lobbying" will become much more powerful in the twenty-first century because of the ease with which issues can be publicized and the more intense convictions of the protesters. This twenty-first-century "new morality" will grow ever stronger and underpin the Age of Selfish Altruism. Governments will need to take action to put environmental safety nets in place to try to prevent problems and establish a clear code of ethics. Companies must learn how to respond quickly and positively to accusations of ethical impropriety or face serious damage to their business. Companies will find it increasingly difficult to separate their corporate entity from their branded products. Consumers are inextricably binding a corporation and its products into a single responsible entity, and holding both under the same level of scrutiny.

Perhaps because of the adverse publicity and aggressive lobbying activity that it suffered in the past, Nestlé for example seems to have undertaken ethical initiatives globally. Its Nespresso brand has launched an "Ecolaboration" initiative, in which every aspect of the supply chain is addressed, from the growing of coffee beans to the disposal of the capsules used. The aim is to reduce its carbon footprint by 20 percent within four years. Equally importantly, Nestlé is working with 80,000 coffee farmers to show them how to use less fertilizer and increase yield. By 2013, it expects to get 80 percent of its coffee from farmers who meet sustainability requirements set out by the environmental group, Rainforest Alliance. Who'd have thought we'd ever see Nestlé and Rainforest Alliance working together?

Perhaps not to be outdone, Lipton Tea now promotes itself in a corporate campaign in Australia as "the world's first Rainforest Alliance Certified tea" and proudly displays its credentials and relationship with its farmers. Nestlé in the Middle East has partnered with the Pan-Arab Osteoporosis Society to increase knowledge and awareness of bone degra-dation problems and encourage preventative action. Nestlé has developed a "pro-bones" milk powder for women with additional nutrients to help develop strong bones, as well as providing financial and logistic support for the Osteoporosis Society. Although this is obviously a marketing strategy to increase milk-powder sales, it links Nestlé with a social cause and improves perceptions of its good corporate citizenship. This is exactly the sort of marketing tactic that will become a common feature of the Age of Selfish Altruism.

Nestlé India has reduced water usage by 70 percent by reusing waste water in its factory boilers, and is using waste nut shells and coffee husks as alternative fuels. All these initiatives are to "get ahead of the curve" and place the company firmly in the camp of ethical citizenship and moral correctness. The old days of a company seeing its sole mandate as simply maximizing the return to shareholders are over. Every corporation now needs to demonstrate its social credentials or face the wrath of its customers and legislators. A company won't be seen only as a money-making business, but it will have to demonstrate its good corporate citizenship by contributing to a better situation in the areas in which it operates. Any CEO claiming that his or her sole responsibility is maximizing returns to the shareholders of his company will be very much out of step with the new morality of the twenty-first century.

Ethical Companies

Companies will be expected to exist not only for the benefit of their shareholders, but also for the benefit of their employees, consumers, and the country in which they reside. The products that a company produces will not only need to provide the functional or emotional benefits for which they are manufactured, but will also need to deliver the highest ethical and moral standards in their production. Louis Vuitton advertisements have a baseline that mentions that the company and the celebrity featured in its advertising are both "proud to support The Climate Project." This sort of public statement of intent or commitment will become increasingly important. Consumers will not only expect a company to develop excellent products, but also to demonstrate its commitment to meeting the moral and ethical standards that its customers hold dear.

As pressure increases on companies to align with certain social causes, it will also affect the products they develop and the way they market their brands. Companies will have to stay true to their social commitment, or face severe criticism if they show any hypocrisy or lack of moral fiber. It will not be enough simply to support a cause through a financial donation. A company will need to *prove* its belief through specific actions related to its products and processes. So if Louis Vuitton does support the ideals of The Climate Project, it will need to ensure that its entire operations are carbon neutral. It will also need to help its employees and the communities in which it operates to reduce their carbon footprint, and demand the same standards from its suppliers and partners. Paying lip service to environmental causes will not cut the mustard with consumers in the future. The days of easy support of social causes will soon be over for businesses, and a need to "live the commitment" will become central to the way companies operate.

The raw capitalism of the past century will moderate into more of a social capitalism, as companies are seen as more than just producers and revenue earners. They will become corporate citizens with the same social responsibilities and moral values as their customers. These corporate changes are being driven by a shift in consumer attitudes and values.

The new morality will affect what people buy and why they buy, and it will increasingly affect both retailers and manufacturers. The new morality of the twenty-first century will play a significant role in consumer decision making. Manufacturers must be prepared to answer much deeper questions about the origins of their products and any damage caused in their production. Retailers must educate their sales staff to respond to ethical questions from consumers about the products they are selling.

We already see many products saying that they were made with recycled paper, or are biodegradable. This is the sort of reassurance that will increasingly need to be provided in the future by virtually all manufacturers, but with a much stronger and clearer commitment.

> *The bottom line for marketers is that consumers are becoming more eager to demonstrate conspicuous virtue than conspicuous consumption.*
> —JWT Trendletter

The New Twenty-First-Century Post-Consumer Society

11

The ideals which have lighted me on my way and time after time given me new courage to face life cheerfully have been Truth, Goodness, and Beauty.

The ordinary objects of human endeavor—property, outward success, luxury—have always seemed to me contemptible.

—Albert Einstein

The Age of Selfish Altruism will create a new generation of "post-consumers." Increasingly, we are choosing to distinguish between what we need and what we want. We want to buy whatever is necessary to maintain or improve our lifestyle, but we don't need to simply keep buying just for the sake of it. We want to maintain or increase our self-esteem, but we are coming to realize that we need to apply some limits. Conspicuous consumption is already being frowned upon in many developed markets, especially in these times of economic pressure. Consumption for its own sake will increasingly be seen as environmentally harmful and ethically irresponsible in the future. Recent financial and economic shocks have added impetus to the general feeling that "enough is enough."

Post-consumers will buy fewer goods, and what they do buy will need to be longer lasting and have real value. Increasingly, the purchase of any product or service will be formed first by the question "do I really need it?" The buying process will become a little more complex and involve greater rationalization. This is not to say that people won't buy something for purely emotional feel-good reasons, but the purchase decision will be considered within the overall context of generally "responsible" buying behavior.

A study in the US by Information Resources Inc. (IRI), identified "a new 'consumer equilibrium' . . . in which behaviors initially implemented to weather the storm have the potential to last well beyond an economic recovery." IRI found that a very large proportion of consumers in all income brackets were changing their definition of what is essential in their lives and buying habits. It seems that conspicuous consumption is becoming a feature of the last century for the population of developed countries. A more complex, perhaps "virtuous" consumption is now beginning to dominate buying behavior. This is clearly a result of the big trends that are affecting consumers, notably a new morality and sense of ethics, plus a greater sense of community and responsibility. But most importantly it seems that the "post-consumers" are developing a different set of needs. They seem to be less focused on the need for self-esteem and status, and more on the need to feel the satisfaction of doing the "right thing" and acting in an ethically sound manner.

The Hierarchy of Needs

Why this profound change in consumer needs and behavior? The change fits precisely into a theory of human needs and aspirations developed by psychologist Abraham Maslow. He hypothesized that there is a hierarchy

Figure 11.1 Maslow's hierarchy of needs

of human needs, and only when certain basic needs are fulfilled can we move on to satisfy "higher needs." Maslow graphically portrayed this "hierarchy of needs" in the form of a pyramid with five different levels (see figure 11.1). The broad base of the pyramid is formed by the "physiological needs" of breathing, sleep, food, water, shelter, and clothing. Above that is the need for "safety and security," which includes a place to live, social stability, health, and employment. The next level of Maslow's pyramid is "love and belonging," which reflects the need for sexual intimacy, family, friendship, and sense of connection. It is perhaps this basic need that is being so well tapped by social networks and other community activities. Only when all these basic human needs have been fulfilled do we reach the aspiration for "self-esteem," which includes confidence, achievement, the respect of others, status, dominance, and prestige. This "self-esteem" level of the pyramid explains obsession with conspicuous consumption. Once we fulfill all our other more basic needs, we move into a self-oriented lifestyle driven by the desire to raise our self-esteem and status. This becomes easier with greater affluence. So the greater the economic development of a country or society, and the broader the middle class, the more self-esteem becomes a powerful driver of human behavior.

The twentieth century saw many countries, especially in Europe and North America, reach a level of affluence that helped them satisfy all their basic needs and focus more directly on satisfying their aspiration for status, social approbation, and self-esteem through conspicuous consumption. Many other countries around the world are reaching a similar stage of development, if not throughout their entire population, certainly among the significant middle class, which is rapidly emerging. This developing nation middle class is now in the full thrill of conspicuous consumption as they flaunt their newfound affluence and confidence. But how long will that last?

There is a fifth and final level of human need, which Maslow calls "self-actualization." This is the top of the needs hierarchy and includes creativity, acceptance of facts, problem solving, meaning and inner potential, and most importantly, morality. It is this level that individuals and societies enter when they feel they have fulfilled their other basic needs, including self-esteem. The need for self-actualization is now influencing the populations of developed countries, and is the reason that conspicuous consumption is being replaced by a much more considered buying process. This is why we are moving from conspicuous consumption to a new society of post-consumers, who have different values. *It is an underlying reason for the Age of Selfish Altruism.*

Maslow's hierarchy of needs clearly shows how conspicuous consumption helps people meet their need for self-esteem, status, and respect, which is a perfectly normal and logical progression in human development. After people have met their more basic needs, they want to acquire the goods and trappings of "success" that allow them to feel greater self-esteem and self-worth. Brands that offer to be a "symbol of your success" or tell you "because you're worth it" are helping consumers meet this need. These are the right sort of marketing and advertising cues for societies that are primarily concerned with self-esteem and remain devoted to conspicuous consumption. However, once we move into the area of post-consumer self-actualization, these same claims can feel really out of touch with the new reality.

Reaching the Peak

A basic level of self-esteem has already been achieved in most developed countries and increasing evidence points to the fact that their populations are now placing greater emphasis on self-actualization, whereas "developing" nations are still enjoying the consumer boom that occurs with new affluence and the deeply rooted desire to satisfy their need for self-esteem.

How long before they move on toward self-actualization will depend on the pace at which they acquire all the possessions they desire, and gain the approbation they crave, to fulfill their need for self-esteem. However, even in these developing markets, the "new morality" and desire for ethical and safe products are having a great influence on purchase behavior. So even their present conspicuous consumption is less selfish and unconcerned than that of the consumers in developed nations in the past.

At some stage, people in all societies go beyond self-esteem to self-actualization, and from conspicuous consumption to post-consumerism. In the past it may have been more a function of age than income. When people reach a certain age, they place less emphasis on the brands and products of self-esteem and become more committed to "second-life" activities. These often involve learning, creativity, and new experiences, which are all classic ways to meet the need for self-actualization. Older people go on international cruises not just because they have the time and money, but because they enjoy learning about, seeing, and meeting new people. They want a more fulfilling life. It is the same when "wrinklies" like my late mother took up pottery classes, tai chi, go back to college, or work in charity shops. They are looking for a new personal fulfillment and inner satisfaction.

Nowadays, it is becoming clearer that people of *every* age in developed countries are saying "enough already." They have acquired the trappings of success and have built sufficient self-esteem, so now they want to move to a "higher" level of self-actualization and morality. The top of Maslow's hierarchy of needs pyramid is the domain of ethical standards and new morality. It is also where the Age of Selfish Altruism resides. Only when people have satisfied their basic need for self-esteem will they enter the new Age of Selfish Altruism.

This is not to say that people no longer want self-esteem; of course they do. None of the levels of Maslow's needs hierarchy disappear after they have been achieved, and they all continue to be needs humans aspire to and hold on to. Every need exists in some form or other in every human, but Maslow's hierarchy of needs theory is expressed as a pyramid, and requires greater security at its base before more emphasis can be given to the higher needs at its apex. So the "luxury" of self-actualization can only become well developed after all the other needs have been solidly satisfied.

The Post-consumer Ethos

Different societies are moving up Maslow's pyramid at different speeds, but with growing global affluence and maturing societies there is an inexorable shift toward self-actualization and an Age of Selfish Altruism. Consumerism and the need for self-esteem will not disappear. People will still value expensive, brand-name goods that increase their status and quality of life, and give them emotional satisfaction. However, value for money and ethical factors will be a *much* stronger part of the purchase equation as the postconsumer society takes hold. Value is the relationship between price and perceived quality.

Post-consumers will ask four basic questions before they buy:

- Do I really need it?

- Does it work perfectly and meet my needs?

- Is it worth the money?

- Does it do no harm?

Manufacturers, and retailers, will need to consider each of these questions or face declining business among post-consumers. The order in which the questions are asked depends on the product category. For example, car buyers may well start with question 4, whereas handbag purchases could start with question 2. Bag, shoe, clothing, and jewelry manufacturers, for example, will need to make their advertising work a lot harder than simply showing vacuous models in strange poses wearing their product. They need to demonstrate a new functionality and relevance, and provide ethical reassurance.

The current Louis Vuitton advertising campaign is an excellent example. It uses well-known, diverse celebrities who are known for their personal integrity such as Keith Richards, Sean Connery, and Francis Ford Coppola with his daughter Sophia. The function, durability, and quality of Vuitton's bags are all clearly displayed along with their owners in widely differing environments, from a hotel room in New York, to a safari in Africa. The bags fit perfectly with the needs of the owner and the different situations they are in. This campaign communicates functionality with integrity, and through the use of celebrities and superb art direction creates powerful aspirational values. This campaign answers the first two and possibly three questions.

But does it do no harm? Every Vuitton ad now makes the claim that the celebrity and the company support The Climate Project. All the boxes are ticked.

Companies will be held increasingly responsible for replacing what they use in the course of manufacture:

- If you use a tree, you need to plant one to replace it.

- If you kill an animal, you need to breed a new one to replace it.

- If you pick food produce, you need to plant new seeds to replace it.
- If you issue emissions you need to compensate or offset the damage they create.

Companies will need to demonstrate their morality and ethical standards in the future or face loss of business. Companies that fail to understand the new post-consumer will suffer. Companies continuing to claim that their product is "a symbol of your success" will likely suffer a slow, but inexorable decline as the message becomes less relevant to more people. The claim will come to be seen as increasingly vacuous by post-consumers and out of step with the Age of Selfish Altruism.

The Need for Humility

Selfish altruism demands a certain amount of humility, as we balance our own aspirations with our sense of ethics. The watch company Patek Philippe has a long-running ad campaign, which perhaps understands this new demand for real value. The ads have the headline, "You never really own a Patek Philippe, you merely look after it for the next generation." This campaign reflects the values of post-consumers in the Age of Selfish Altruism, who will search for genuine quality and real value within the context of "doing what's right." Quality will replace quantity as a primary motivator. Long-lasting value and real values will be far more important than transient pleasure.

In much of Asia, there is a Confucian ethic that demands humility despite success, and the appearance of simple living despite great wealth. When I lived in Taiwan, my landlord, Mr. Cheng, wore tattered pants, a rather smelly old zip-up windcheater, and a weathered baseball cap. He rode a rusty old motorbike, and frankly, looked a bit like a tramp. I later discovered that he not only owned all the houses on the street, but several office buildings. The man must have been a many times multimillionaire, but he obviously felt it would not be "proper" to show this wealth. I came across this same perspective many times in Asia. The wealthiest people would tell me that no matter how rich they were they still only needed three meals a day to survive. Of course, they privately enjoyed the luxuries that affluence afforded them, but they were reluctant to "show off" their wealth in public.

These Confucian attitudes have been eroded in China and across many countries in Asia with the sudden affluence that has been created in the past 20 years. Fast, easy money has spawned the same need for self-aggrandizement that Western markets felt in the 1980s and 1990s. Nouveau riche people display ego-polishing flashiness with rather bad taste. The traditional observance of filial piety with the responsibility of care for one's parents and extended family has been increasingly eroded and seen as less important than personal welfare. This trend is understandable as young people have the affluence and seek the self-esteem of buying their own apartment and living an independent, successful life. They have enough pressure to achieve their goals without also having to care for their parents, grandparents, brothers, sisters, cousins, uncles, and aunties. However, the old values may well reassert themselves as East Asian countries continue to grow more affluent. We are seeing a new wave of people in developed Asian countries who want to be appreciated for the person they are, rather than recognized for what they are.

The fate of Mercedes-Benz is a good reflection of the change from self-esteem to self-actualization. Mercedes has always been seen as a "symbol of your success." In Asia, rich factory managers and the affluent founders of businesses all drove Mercedes, and most still do. Along with XO cognac and Rolex, a Mercedes demanded recognition and respect. These symbols of success continue to thrive with the growth of the economies and spreading affluence. But from Taiwan to Singapore, and India to China, a new type of car buyer is emerging. He or she wants a high-quality, reliable car, but it needs to be *less conspicuous*. He or she is happy to pay a lot of money for the car, but doesn't want to display having done so. He or she wants all the satisfaction that money can bring, but doesn't seek to flaunt it. The main beneficiaries of this trend have been brands such as Audi and Lexus, which offer quality and good taste without being too conspicuous. These brands are more focused on inner satisfaction than outward showiness.

Marketing to the Post-consumer

Mercedes is still seen as the most prestigious car to own, but it is in a battle to make its brand image more appealing to this new generation of post-consumers as it gradually loses its market leadership. All the indications are that even in Asia, as people satisfy their need for self-esteem, the leading-edge "affluents" are already moving toward the need for self-actualization.

This new twenty-first-century morality and sense of ethical responsibility will reignite a greater appreciation of extended family and acceptance of social obligation. The global trend toward community and collaboration and the need for self-actualization will strengthen the family unit as well as underpin culture, learning, uplifting experiences, and even religion. Confucian values are likely to reassert themselves in Asia, just as other morality- and community-based ethics have reemerged elsewhere in the world. They may not always be described as Confucian, Buddhist, Hindu, Christian, or Muslim, but those same values of moderation, kindness to others, and community spirit will increasingly come to the fore globally. People will search to find greater meaning in life, and seek to make the most of their lives.

A key challenge for marketers will be to understand the new values of these post-consumers in the Age of Selfish Altruism. Post-consumers of the twenty-first century are more likely to:

- buy clothes and consumer items that are well made and have lasting value;
- look for valuable heirlooms, not just fashionable, bling watches and jewelry;
- purchase long-lasting electric cars that don't guzzle gas or need to be constantly serviced;
- pay a premium to fly on aircraft that have no carbon emissions; stay at eco-friendly hotels that bring income and a better quality of life to the local population, and are committed to protecting the flora and fauna;
- prefer food that has an ethical "source tag" confirming where it came from and how it was produced;
- dedicate greater expenditure to beauty products, especially items related to anti-aging. However, there will be a clear preference for natural products, brands that haven't been animal tested, and companies that have demonstrated environmental responsibility;
- buy solar-powered housing with an eco-friendly design, a family entertainment room, adequate guest and extended family accommodation, communications center, and a home gym.

Sadly, being an aging population, they will feel the need for self-esteem, so facelifts and cosmetic surgery will be as important in the twenty-first century as designer bags and great shoes were in the past century. Teeth whitening will be the new bling!

As people get older they apply different criteria to what they purchase. They make value decisions about what new purchases will mean to their life; not only the practical value, but also the contribution a purchase will make to their lifestyle and sense of satisfaction.

The evidence is that older people are choosing:

- experiences and lifestyle over materialism

- lasting value over short-term excitement

- real quality over ephemeral fashion.

Research from a company called Silver shows that increasing one's mental and physical wellbeing is regarded by older people as much more important than acquiring new goods and assets. Spending by older people is reallocated from buying consumer goods to buying experiences, finding "enlightenment," and maintaining a healthy, youthful appearance. This rejection of traditional product consumerism isn't related to lack of wealth, it is brought about by a fundamental change of values with increasing age, which creates strong "post-consumerist" behavior.

Friends become far more important than status, and a lot of effort is put into social activities and staying in touch. Aging post-consumers are highly "value and values" driven, so it could be argued that aging "boomers" are yet again setting trends, or at the very least amplifying new trends and values in the new Age of Selfish Altruism.

12

The Age of Selfish Altruism

I arise in the morning torn between a desire to improve the world and a desire to enjoy the world.

—E.B. White, author

The challenge for the twenty-first century is the balance between wanting to do what is best for yourself and ensuring that you live up to your ethical and moral standards.

This is *selfish altruism*: the desire to buy for yourself—but ensure that you're not causing any collateral damage.

To do what's best for yourself—but ensure you don't do any harm to the environment, ecology or other people.

The aspiration to benefit yourself—combined with an urge to help others at the same time.

Selfish altruism is based on a growing belief that we're all in this together. The actions of each individual will affect many others.

Research by market consultancy Mext in Australia found that people are becoming much more demanding and opinionated. Mext's researchers found that people are thinking much more long term, and are very concerned about sustainability and a cohesive society. The key findings of this research have also emerged in similar studies in many other countries, and they indicate that stronger values and a commitment to environmental sustainability are becoming central tenets in our lives. Most importantly, the Mext research indicated that Generation Y in particular are now changing, " . . . from mindless consumption to consuming mindfully." This is a wonderful definition of the new Age of Selfish Altruism.

We will gradually transition away from the Consumer Century with its conspicuous consumption driven by self-esteem to an Age of Selfish Altruism with more considered and considerate purchasing. After generations of conspicuous consumption, we won't kick our addiction to shopping or lose the enjoyment of buying interesting goods. The social and lifestyle benefits of shopping expeditions bring great pleasure to many people, and the desire to increase self-esteem will always exist. It is therefore likely that people won't go shopping any less often, and that is good news for all retailers. However, the *way* people buy, and *what* they buy, will change along with their values and attitudes.

Trendspotter Marian Salzman at Porter Novelli talks about the importance of "value and values." She says that: "Value used to mean lots more for the price: bigger, faster, brighter, more features, more prestige. But the greedy rise of 'more' has hit a ceiling. The commercial reality is that cautious consumers seek a new kind of value." She goes on to say, "In 2009 and beyond, watch for consensus building around values that suddenly feel so much more important: stability, sustainability, cooperation, and peace of mind."

Conspicuous consumption was driven by the need for self-esteem, with little regard for its implications or impact. Selfish altruism balances personal need with a new mindful consideration. We aren't all becoming "bleeding hearts," or changing from heartless capitalists to social workers. Nor will we suddenly shift from one kind of buying system to another. It is simply that we are learning a new balance in our decision making, which will influence what we buy and how we buy. Even economist Paul Krugman agrees, and says "I am not overflowing with human compassion. It's more of an intellectual thing. I don't buy that selfishness is always good. That doesn't fit the way the world works."

The growing concern and consensus about the need for global action on climate change is contributing to a broader morality and sense of ethics. In addition, the growth of online social networking has created a new feeling of "global empowerment." Social networking sites have become a key feature of the Age of Selfish Altruism. Perhaps this is why the most important, overwhelming sentiment driving selfish altruism will be—*it's up to we!* I want what's best for me, but at the same time *we* should all try to help others. I want to buy whatever I desire, but it cannot be at the cost of others, because *we* are all in this together. This is the Age of Selfish Altruism.

An article in *The Times* newspaper was headlined, "We've decided to care again," and reported that Britons are becoming less selfish and placing greater emphasis on environmental and world affairs. It went on to say, "The middle-classes have questioned their core values more than any other social grouping, with 27% admitting to reassessing their outlook." A third of the group surveyed claimed they were now more concerned about their families. A significant minority insisted they are committed to buying from ethical companies. And a staggering 41 percent claimed they will place less importance on material possessions when the recession ends.

This has huge implications for marketers, because it will not be business as usual when the economy recovers. It will be the Age of Selfish Altruism. No one believes there will be easy answers or fast solutions to the world's problems, but there is a strong desire for change and a growing sense of frustration.

JWT published a report called "The Collective Consciousness," which "speaks to a new global mindset: people are thinking less about "me" and more about what "we" can do together—whether for pure fun, for sharing resources, or for tackling global issues like climate change." The study found that "people are pooling resources, sharing ideas and coordinating actions as never before."

The root of this new collective consciousness is based upon two fundamentals: the desire and ability to join communities, and the ease with which this can now be accomplished; and the realization that collectively driven solutions can be found for large-scale problems. JWT identifies "a new generation's desire and ability to communicate, exchange ideas, and organize collectively."

The study found that experimentation and innovation are flourishing as people integrate their online and offline activities to carry out collective goals. "Today's overwhelming issues can be addressed only through widespread collaboration with a 'we' rather than 'me' mentality. There is a growing realization that we're all in this together."

We're not going to shake off the selfish legacy of the twentieth century easily, and the desire to do what's best for oneself will continue to underpin our behavior and actions in the near term. But the cynicism of the past century is already converting into a criticism of anyone who is not doing their part to support agreed communal values. Once *we* all sign up to take action, or are forced to do so, we will not tolerate others "cheating" or being irresponsible or unethical. Every individual and every company must play a part in achieving the goals we all agreed for the greater good. Selfish altruism will be the defining characteristic of twenty-first-century behavior: doing what's best for ourselves *and* everyone else.

Selfish altruism will manifest itself across society, business, and politics to create a new set of dynamics based on a greater social awareness and sense of what's right for the individual, as well as the community. We may not all really be socialists now, as *Newsweek* recently proclaimed, but *we* are developing a great new sense of social responsibility, morality, and ethics. Welcome to the Age of Selfish Altruism!

New Environmentalism

Selfish altruism demands acceptance of social responsibility, and this will be a leading attitudinal dynamic and key pillar of twenty-first-century morality. The demand for social responsibility will govern politics, business and personal life. Here's what the UK's Green Party's Sian Berry said in her criticism of "disposable fashion": "Clothes are made from precious resources. Polyester is made from fossil fuels and cotton is a very land- and water-intensive crop. A lot of chemicals are also used on the crop, which will contaminate the land and leak into the water supply. If someone wears that garment to a few parties then chucks it in the bin, all that environmental damage has gone into filling up a hole in the ground." Right now we might think Sian's comments as being a bit over the top, but they contain insights into the new morality of selfish altruism.

I believe that what she is saying will quickly become accepted as mainstream thought. Sian's perspective will come to increasingly affect purchase patterns across most product categories. Not all of a sudden, but slowly and naturally. The awareness and concern about environmental damage caused in the production of clothing, or any other product, will become part of mainstream thought, and a critical element in future consumer purchasing. This is environmentalism in the Age of Selfish Altruism.

Additional pressure on "disposable clothing" is being applied by the charity War on Want, which also criticizes "cheap chic" on the basis of the treatment of the people who make it. How can a store make a profit on items of $5 clothing unless someone has been paid a pittance to make it? It published a report called "Fashion Victims," which exposed the abuse and pitiful pay of Bangladeshi garment workers. Again, Sian Berry has the last word, "We'd like to see people spending a bit more on clothes they really love."

I couldn't have expressed it better. This is exactly the consumer attitude that I believe will become more and more prevalent as the century progresses. Businesses are already recognizing the needs of the Age of Selfish Altruism, and are designing business models to meet our new moral standards. The Fair Trade movement, for example, marries concern for the planet, with the welfare of its inhabitants. Fair Trade products are the result of social contracts with producers in which growers of coffee, for example, are guaranteed a minimum payment, which will ensure that they have a sustainable and healthy lifestyle. Consumers usually have to pay a little extra for the coffee, but are prepared to do so to ensure a sustainable world for everyone. Fair Trade is the precursor of many more commercial contracts between what we want and the way we want it.

There are lots of things we want to buy, but we want to ensure that *everyone benefits* when we spend our money with a retailer or e-tailer. We want to benefit ourselves *and* the retailer that sold us the product; the manufacturer *and* its employees, the grower and producer of the raw materials *and* the earth itself. This is marketing in the Age of Selfish Altruism.

New websites are springing up that allow us to be selfishly altruistic without any real effort. Online shopping portal www.smartlygreen.com, for example, enables online shoppers to help the environment without making any changes to their lifestyle, and without any extra cost. The site provides a portal through which users can access their normal online shopping outlets. It costs no more for the users, but smartlygreen.com gets a commission from the retailers for delivering a shopper, which it then contributes to an organization that helps protect rainforests, which are the "lungs" of our world. The consumer can help save the planet, and companies can demonstrate their CSR commitment, all with very little extra effort. This is the Age of Selfish Altruism made easy! It's up to "we" to make a difference, but it's up to companies to help us achieve our goals.

Businesses that provide all the functional attributes that consumers demand of their products, *and* deliver values and benefits that allow buyers to feel morally good about themselves will be big winners this century. Moral or ethical benefits don't have to be a key selling point for every product, but are most likely to be a basis for reassurance and emotional satisfaction that the Age of Selfish Altruism demands. Companies that understand this underlying morality and the need to provide whatever ethical reassurance the buyer is looking for will be much better grounded for success this century.

Nike "dryfit" sports shirts offer a specific functionality that helps keep the body dry during sports activities, and this is the reason that athletes buy the product. However, the shirt also carries a little tag that says:

Regenerated Content.

Materials generated from pre-consumer and post-consumer waste have been used to manufacture this garment.

To learn more about our regenerated product initiatives please visit www.considereddesign.com

Nike has always based its business model on "real values" and performance improvement, not simply image or appearance. However, Nike clearly understands the emerging Age of Selfish Altruism, by adding value through the assurance of ethical and environmental responsibility. The brand wants to help you to achieve your personal health and fitness goals, but not at the cost of others or the environment.

The reaction of my colleague who bought the shirt was interesting. When he first read the tag he was appalled that he had paid all that money to wear a product made of waste. It sounded quite repulsive. But when he thought about it, he felt a warm glow of satisfaction that he was playing his part in a recycling, waste-free world. He felt that Nike understood him better than any other manufacturer of sports shirts, and he has since become much more brand loyal. This is the altruistic sentiment of the Age of Selfish Altruism.

Individuals will voluntarily do whatever they can to meet their selfish altruistic standards, as long as it doesn't greatly inconvenience them or cost way too much extra money. Companies must do their part in meeting the social and environmental expectations of their consumers, by producing goods or services which meet the needs of this new twenty-first-century morality.

Selfish Altruism in Action

However, it is likely that most of the voluntary action taken will only be "baby steps" toward the objectives that people of the twenty-first century have in mind, especially environmental. If big strides are to be taken, they almost certainly will need to be mandated by government policy. There are only two ways to create *major* changes in behavior: the carrot and the stick.

The "carrot" option delivers change that is painless and seamless so that people hardly realize it's happening. The "stick" simply mandates change and punishes anyone failing to adhere to the new standards. "Carrots" are usually forms of legislation that reward customers or companies through grants or tax exemptions. For example, individuals are already enjoying subsidies for electric car purchase, or exempted from inner city congestion charges when driving an eco-friendly vehicle. For companies, carrots would include tax deductions which may be based on the type of manufacturing materials used, emission standards, and health benefits for their employees. This introduction of "carrots" to induce behavioral change is already happening, and has little affect on the lifestyle of consumers, who enjoy all the functional improvements, financial benefits, emotional rewards, and moral satisfaction without any personal pain. The "stick" method inflicts pain, and usually demands a considerable change of lifestyle or personal sacrifice.

Perhaps the best example of a big stick already being felt by most households in the developed world is in their garbage collection. In the effort to achieve a cleaner, sustainable environment, and reduce landfill, governments are mandating separation of materials to allow easy recycling. Separate bins must be used to contain paper versus plastic, metals, biodegradables and other refuse. Homeowners with gardens are being induced to throw biodegradable foodstuffs and natural materials on garden compost heaps. The amount of waste per household is also being limited. One bin per household per week is becoming the norm. If a household wants a second bin, it pays a significant extra price to its local authority. Demanding the separation of different materials to allow recycling, plus restrictions on the volume of garbage allowed and the frequency of its collection have *forced* households to change their behavior. This is probably the first mandated action to help the environment that has really affected a consumer's lifestyle. And it is being aggressively enforced.

Only when governments force big changes in human behavior or lifestyle will it ever happen. Governments are now going further by banning plastic bags and mandating packaging changes. Pretty soon, we'll have to eat the packaging after we've consumed the product. And I don't want to think about waste separation after that!

Voluntourism

There is an increasing belief that we all need to do what we can to help, and if that coincides with something we want to buy or do, it meets both our selfish and altruistic needs. "Voluntourism" is one the clearest manifestations and easiest ways to capitalize on selfish altruism. The desire to satisfy one's own "self-actualization" need to learn and do more, combined with the ability to help others or play some sort of role in improving the world. John F. Kennedy started the Peace Corps in the US, and now Barack Obama is again urging Americans to serve the communities in which they live, and engage with the world at large—to go out and do good.

Most Western countries have some sort of overseas volunteer program that has been a part of many people's lives before or after college. But increasingly professionals are taking time off work, or engaging in volunteer work after they retire. Others who can't retire or take extended time away from work are finding that "voluntourism" combines a holiday with some worthy work overseas. Most of the programs involve ecology or wildlife conservation, or social programs involving teaching, building or farming. Many "volunteering" holidays are simply interesting vacations with some token engagement thrown in, while other programs are real commitments that also allow you to see other cultures and lifestyles. They can be as short as a few weeks or extend for a couple of years, and involve some hard work. If the idea of actually working on a vacation is a problem, there are a myriad of new hotels and holidays which are designed to help the local community or improve the environment. Or both. I remember the many signs I have read over the years on various beaches, asking us to "Take only photos, leave only footprints in the sand." Now voluntourism allows us take greater pleasure and leave behind a more positive footprint.

If you are a marketer involved in any kind of tourism or travel-related business, you'd be wise to look for altruistic "add-ons." Even the smallest actions can add a new dimension to your customer's experience, generate repeat business, improve your CSR program, and develop your own sense of satisfaction. It's a win–win opportunity. This is travel and vacations in the Age of Selfish Altruism.

Philanthropy

This same sense of ethics is also emerging in the area of philanthropy, with social media being the enabler. Again, Marian Salzman at Porter Novelli identified "the rise of the $104/year donor." She explains that: "[I]t's the new philanthropy . . . the power to make real moves via laptop or BlackBerry or iPhone, via small donations that gain strength from the momentum of massive virtual networks." Marian talks about people blogging and tweeting about the causes they care about. "They delight in daily debates with those who share their passion . . . and the satisfaction of constantly connecting with their community." These people get to see the instant results of their efforts "whether it's organizing a rally via Twitter, spreading awareness by recruiting new members on Facebook, or watching their donations tote up the tally another notch."

An example she quoted was Twestival, an event spanning 202 cities around the world organized over Twitter, a fast, free, simple way to connect with like-minded people. This event raised more than a quarter of a million dollars from across a multitude of people, in a wide variety of countries, in a single day, to fund clean-water projects in Africa.

Although "voluntourism" and online philanthropy are the most obvious *mass* manifestation of the new twenty-first-century morality, we see individuals displaying the same dedication to selfish altruism. Most hospitals, libraries, universities, schools, museums, research institutions, and sports arenas, and many government edifices have wings or entire buildings named after wealthy benefactors. When a person has accumulated great wealth, he or she soon passes through the simple ego satisfaction and moves toward generous actions that bring personal and public reward. Paying for the construction of a fine building and naming it after you have always been a wonderful combination of boosting the donor's self-esteem with a need for problem solving, morality, and creativity.

From the beginning of time individuals who have accumulated great wealth took this path of selfish altruism: from Roman emperors to kings and queens, and industrialists to bankers. However, many very rich people are now going beyond the construction of buildings into a new form of personal charitable giving called "philanthrocapitalism." The Bill and Melinda Gates Foundation is one of the largest private charitable foundations in the world. One of the primary aims of the foundation is to improve health care and reduce extreme poverty globally, and to improve educational standards. The Gateses believe that hunger, preventable disease and lack of education is immoral in today's world, but they are in a unique position to make a difference. They have convinced Warren Buffett that this is morally the right thing to do, and he has agreed to contribute his billions to helping achieve the foundation's goals.

This is a type of commitment we will see more of in the twenty-first century. It allows individuals who have high moral standards to use their money and abilities to make a difference. The key difference versus charities in the past is that venture philanthropies are run like a business with clear metrics for success, professional managers, and constant performance reviews. The new morality of the twenty-first century isn't just wishful thinking, and hoping for the best, it is all about *making it happen*.

I played a very small part in helping the launch of The Community Foundation of Singapore. It allows affluent people to donate to charity but specify exactly where and how they want their money to be applied. The Community Foundation then manages the program and provides regular updates, status reports and results analysis. A donor can target a specific area for attention and have his or her funds applied to improve the situation. If donors wish, they can name the program after themselves, their parents, or even their dog. If you have some serious money, this is a much more satisfying way to donate than simply giving funds to a charity and hoping it is spent wisely. Big charities are therefore increasingly likely to acquire most of their funds from many millions of smaller donations, rather like a supermarket. And the specialty "philanthrocapitalist" charities can personally manage fewer, larger donations, like an upmarket boutique. These are philanthropy and charity in the Age of Selfish Altruism.

Government legislation will be used as a stronger tool in the Age of Selfish Altruism. The reason for this will be that consensus decisions will be made with the best of motives, but simply hoping for voluntary participation will not be an option. Individual responsibility for sustainability will be something that we all believe in, and we will do whatever we can to personally live up to this credo. But "doing what we can" will soon not be enough.

Action to prevent global warming, and encourage sustainability, will become so important to entire nations, that hoping for individual, voluntary action will not be sufficient to achieve the goals which have been set. Very aggressive carrot and stick legislation will soon be enacted to force major changes in behavior, and individual adherence to the laws will be taken very seriously indeed. This is because failure to accept individual responsibility in the drive to achieve a sustainable lifestyle may result in the collective failure of a society or country to meet the standards that it has committed to on a global basis. National failure could result in economic sanctions and exclusion from the global community of nations.

A recent article in the *New York Times*, by the economist Paul Krugman, raised the likelihood of economic sanctions against China if it goes ahead with its plans to build several new coal-fired power stations. The impact of the carbon dioxide from these new power stations would nullify the emission-reduction efforts of most other nations. China is already the biggest carbon dioxide producer in the world, and to allow such massive increases in new emissions over the next few years must inevitably draw the ire of other nations. As the US, EU, Japan, and many other nations pay the economic price for their own carbon dioxide reductions, they will hold the moral high ground to take punitive action against those who continue to increase emissions.

So Krugman predicts a carbon tax on China-made goods levied by the US, and presumably by the EU. This is the kind of punishment that an entire country could suffer if its population fails to meet individual standards of sustainability. Could the twenty-first century see the first serious international conflicts over environmental issues? This would be a logical extension of the wars over trade and property that occurred in the past two centuries when greed and selfish national interest are given higher priority over the planet and the world's population. It is therefore inevitable that we will see aggressive new sustainability laws passed in the next decade that change building codes, transportation, and all categories of personal power usage. Governments will get very tough indeed on anyone who fails to meet the standards set out for each individual. Make no mistake, as countries have to meet stringent environmental standards and reduce carbon emissions, personal freedom will suffer. However, these restrictions will be accepted by the population as being for the "common good." This may worry an aging baby boomer such as me, but it will not worry my grandchildren at all. They will be willing participants in the belief that every individual must be part of the social contract to save the planet and "do what's right." This is the underlying morality of the Age of Selfish Altruism.

We may all have to make sacrifices and work together to save the planet, but we will need to work very hard to not lose our humanity, individuality, and personal freedoms. The Age of Selfish Altruism will create consensual opinions, and generate new legislation that *we* will demand to achieve our goals. We want to do what's best for ourselves, but at the same time do what's right for everyone. We all play a part voluntarily at present, but in the future we may be simply forced by government diktat to change our lifestyles and deliver help where it is needed. The Age of Selfish Altruism will be a tricky balancing act between selfish individuality and altruistic plurality.

Business in the Age of Selfish Altruism

Social obligation is much bigger than supporting worthy causes.
It includes anything that impacts people and the quality of
their lives.
—William Ford Jr., chairman, Ford Motor Co.

Businesses will need to adapt to the Age of Selfish Altruism. At present most major businesses have a CSR program. They will argue that this is evidence of their altruism and demonstrates their good citizenship. But most CSR programs are simply a sticking plaster on the corporate annual report. They are primarily public relations activities, or opportunities to cut costs. *In the future, CSR will need to be at the heart of a company's operations, and affect every aspect of their business process and product delivery.*

I know from my own experience with major corporations that most CSR initiatives are largely self-serving. They are used to generate positive publicity, or gain a competitive advantage in the marketplace, or reduce costs and increase profits. Actually, all that is terrific, because the biggest corporate inhibitor to improved ethical or environmental standards is cost. Most companies complain that meeting new health and environmental standards will cost them too much money and reduces their efficiency or competitiveness. So any opportunity to generate profit enhancement through environmental improvement will gain immediate traction within a company.

In the past, most companies viewed CSR as primarily a PR opportunity. Then some of these PR opportunities actually reduced costs, and beneficially affected the bottom line. Most hotels now ask you to reuse towels, and allow them to change sheets less regularly to reduce washing and water usage. We go along with this, but we all believe that its main *raison d'être* is to improve hotel profit margins by reducing man hours, wear and tear on sheets and towels, and laundry costs. Or am I being too cynical?

Electricity savings follow a similar pattern, when aircons and lights in a hotel room are only activated by inserting entry cards into the power slot. Yes, it reduces power consumption, but it also significantly reduces the hotel's electricity bill. So we all win. Hotels cut their operating costs and consumers feel they are being environmentally responsible. Jumeirah Hotels is producing an annual corporate responsibility report covering "corporate governance, health and safety, the environment, as well as responsibilities towards colleagues, customers, business partners, owners and the local community." This sort of report will become necessary for all corporations, if it isn't actually mandated by government in the near future.

Coca-Cola is providing a "green allowance" to its employees in the UK, to encourage them to use public transport, and a "carbon challenge" to enlist their help in reducing its carbon footprint. The company has invested in monitors and devices to reduce electricity, gas, and water usage, and hopes to achieve full payback on their investment within a year. In Sri Lanka, Coke has a "Give Back Life" program, which teaches people to collect and recycle PET bottles. This sort of activity has in turn led to greater proactivity within companies to find new business opportunities based on environmental, health, and social platforms. For example, salt reduction in food cuts manufacturing costs, benefits consumers' health, and provides a new "low-sodium" advertising platform to promote the brand. There are a myriad of commercial opportunities for companies that embrace sustainability and understand the selfish altruism of consumers in the twenty-first century.

Greenness as a Sales Tool

We have already forecast the need for companies to disclose the environmental effects of their production or face consumer purchase resistance. The combination of this consumer demand and legislative mandate will put CSR at the very centre of many companies' operations.

New legislation that increases company contributions to employee pensions, health benefits, and welfare provisions will become increasingly onerous. Faced with declining populations, the elimination of the retirement age will become a necessary expedient in Japan, Germany, and other countries faced with workforce shortages. Governments will want people to work longer to ease the pressure on pensions and welfare, and companies will want reliable, professional employees. So the retirement age may simply drift away into the distance as people work pretty much all their lives. Governments will also encourage female employees to have children, and will force companies to allow extensive paid time away from work for both males and females who are building a family. Over the years, pregnancy leave has increased from a few days' absence, to a couple of weeks' leave, to a few months' paid leave, and now to both partners getting extensive leave of a year or more.

However, the biggest impact on companies will be the demand from governments that employers be responsible for maintaining their employees' health and fitness. Aggressive, mandatory health legislation is on its way. Companies will be forced to monitor and keep records of non-invasive statistics such as height, weight, body mass, blood pressure, bone mass, and lung capacity. Almost every developed country will push as much of the onus as possible for fitness and health onto employers.

As health care and medical costs spiral out of control in country after country, governments will push responsibility down to companies and then to individuals themselves. New legislation (hopefully carrot rather than stick) will likely influence the type of food served in canteens, increase the demand for company gyms, and provide paid absences for exercise and keep-fit sessions.

All this new legislation will mean that company CSR and employee welfare won't be voluntary in the twenty-first century, with "doing our very best" objectives. There will be specific KPIs and measurements. Failure to achieve the specific standards set for a company will have severe consequences, rather than the directors being simply "disappointed." Corporate tax grades may well be tied to delivery of key CSR standards in the future. Corporations will be expected to become real citizens of a country, and will be treated in the same way as every other taxpayer. The management and directors of a company will be held personally responsible for ensuring that the company acts in the same way as any citizen of that nation. They will be forced to accept personal, not just corporate, responsibility. Management and directors' personal taxes may be affected as well as the company's if they fail to maintain environmental and health standards, and achieve the CSR goals established.

Companies can use the changes in CSR legislation and employee welfare to deliver competitive advantage and greater profitability if they are intelligent, resourceful, and committed. On a final note, it is important that CSR be used as a business ethos, and not simply as a sales tool. There may be occasions when "greenness" is the primary reason for using a product or service. But in most cases, products and services need to be sold on their own benefits or they will very quickly lose their competitive edge. A very simple example would be a clothes detergent. That the detergent is fully biodegradable, does not contain any pollutants, and is entirely natural may add to its appeal significantly. However, unless it delivers the optimal cleaning performance for which purpose it is purchased, it will not remain viable for long.

Also, consumers are becoming much warier of environmental claims, and instead of adding to a brand's values may actually cause some erosion if the benefits are unclear. A JWT study found that while Australians are increasingly environmentally conscious and concerned about sustainability, the term "green" evokes considerable cynicism. Many consumers regard it as a trendy but ambiguous marketing buzzword. "Green" was the most trademarked term in the US in 2007. JWT concludes that as consumers grow more conscious of "greenwashing," companies will need to speak honestly about tangible actions they have taken, and specifically what benefits accrue to the buyer of its products. Any attempt to simply cloak a business or product in "greenness" will be treated with contempt by consumers. The credibility of any "green" claim will depend on the evidence for the claims being irrefutable.

A senior P&G marketer told his staff that "greenwashing" wasn't a viable competitive platform for any of their products. Being environmentally friendly was a constant goal, and could be an added value, but no brand should move away from its core consumer benefits and values. This is the Age of Selfish Altruism, not just altruism.

A business that makes nothing but money is a poor business.
—Henry Ford

Government in the Age of Selfish Altruism

Democracy is the road to socialism.
—Karl Marx

In the twenty-first century, the role of government will increasingly be that of organizer, litigator, and enforcer of public demands. Governments that endlessly discuss policies and debate actions will increasingly be seen as simply politicians prevaricating on vital issues. Action will be demanded that clearly and effectively solves problems. The frustrations of the populace will need to be addressed, and "action this day" will be the key message for government.

In their haste to take action, governments will occasionally over-step the mark to achieve results and this may well diminish individual rights and freedoms. The Patriot Act in the US is a classic example of rights and freedoms being trampled "for the protection of all." Human rights lawyers and constitutional experts were appalled by the invasive measures of this act. However, the American people accepted new privations and restrictions as being necessary "in the war against terror."

As happened in America, impositions and restrictions on indi-viduals will be seen as an acceptable price to pay to achieve the goals of the populace. It may be antiterrorist activity, environmental require-ments, or social demands that drive new legislation. Whatever the reason, people will sacrifice some personal freedoms if that is what is required to achieve significant results. Individuals will be prepared to accept personal restrictions for the good of all, when forced to do so by government mandate. We all understand that sometimes *we* have to pay a price to get what we want.

Governments will therefore be given greater powers to enact legislation which delivers the levels of social and environmental safety that we will demand. Acceptance of government-mandated restrictions or actions is part of the new morality of the twenty-first century. We will accept various restrictions, or be forced to take certain actions, to achieve a greater good. These restrictions or actions will be accepted because "we" believe that they are in our best interest.

Politically, we are already entering a world of centrist or "left of center" politics. The extremes of left- and right-wing politics created in the nineteenth century probably died in twentieth century after Margaret Thatcher and Ronald Reagan versus the Communist threat. Govern-ments all over the world now have a remarkably similar economic and social perspective as they cater to public opinion and new morality being much more directly expressed. Tony Blair ushered centrist politics into the UK, with his "third way," neither right nor left. The current Conservative Party would see only the slightest of differences if it was led by Tony Blair and his New Labor policies. Both Labor and Conserva-tive have become entirely centrist.

The US has now elected its own "socialist" in the person of Barack Obama, who is taking a bipartisan, centrist, consultative approach in his policies and actions. He wants to ensure that health care is universally available in the US, eliminate poverty, and raise taxes on the rich to pay for social reforms. But he is still pro-business, and committed to individual freedom, personal enterprise and opportunity. Yikes, maybe he's Tony Blair's long lost cousin . . . Equally importantly he is an environmentalist, who is committed to sustainable energy and the radical reduction of carbon emissions.

In India, the Congress Party won the 2009 general election, causing one political commentator to say, "This election is a rejection of both the right and left in favor of a centrist ideology that can walk the tightrope between capitalism and socialism." All over the world we see these same types of centrist government policies. A *Newsweek* magazine cover in January 2009 was headlined "We're all socialist now." That was most prescient, and although it is not entirely accurate, it very much nailed the political outlook for this century as the new social morality and Age of Selfish Altruism become more strongly established.

In the past century, political parties adopted a "sales-driven" approach. They "stood for" certain policies and values. So a Democratic Party or Labor Party had a very different social and political agenda from the Republicans or Conservatives. The effect was that governments lurched from left to right and back again in various cycles according to the mood of the populace. This created lots of uncertainties and policy shifts.

With growing affluence, the middle class grew to become the key to political power in most countries. The middle class wants a delicate balance between social responsibility and individual discretion in this Age of Selfish Altruism. The middle class wants excellent free health care, excellent public services, and welfare payments sufficient to ensure that no one goes without, and is prepared to pay a little extra tax to achieve these ethical goals. It understands that business must prosper to create wealth, so it wants a government that is pro-business, but provides clear ethical guidelines for companies and monitors the quality and safety of their output. Understanding this balance between the selfish and the altruistic has become the key to political survival in most Western democracies.

Political parties have therefore changed from being sales driven to market driven. Governments now find out what the people want, and promise to give it to them. Politicians learned that rather than taking a particular stance and trying to persuade people their particular policies were right, they would simply listen to public opinion and offer up policies that the majority wanted. This is the approach that Tony Blair took to bring his "new" Labor Party back into power after 17 years in the left-wing wilderness. New Labor became so centrist that a significant number of Conservative voters found that Blair offered a social agenda with which they agreed, rather than the more right-wing policies of their own party. Blair even praised Margaret Thatcher for heaven's sake, and proudly built on her economic legacy. The old Labor Party firebrands of the past must have been turning in their graves.

Blair demonstrated that control of the political middle ground was the way to electoral victory. Understanding the new middle-class morality and catering to their ethics and values was the way to retain power. He understood selfish altruism because he believed in it himself. Saint Tony was only unseated when he made decisions about Iraq and military power that were not in keeping with the opinions of the UK populace. He tried the old-style "selling" of a policy to the people instead of asking what they wanted. Big mistake, Tony! I'm sure that much of Blair's thinking on Iraq was ultimately altruistic. He probably truly believed that by removing Saddam he could improve the lot of Iraqis and bring greater calm to a troubled Middle East. However, altruism toward people who have not voted for you is rarely a successful political formula. British voters suffered higher taxes and military casualties, and closed the door on Blair's time as prime minister.

Selfish altruism is very much stronger in countries where there is an affluent middle class. In most developed markets, the general public is now asking for increased social benefits, greater environmental responsibility, and higher ethical standards, so government will need to mandate it. This may have lots of repercussions on the actions demanded of individuals and some infringement of their rights, but the evidence is that people will increasingly sacrifice some personal liberty "for the common good." There is, however, no doubt that governments will become much more intrusive in our lives in the Age of Selfish Altruism.

Democracy gives every man the right to be his own oppressor.
—James Russell Lowell

Health Care in the Age of Selfish Altruism

The greatest wealth is health.
—Virgil

Nowhere will government intrusion be felt more acutely than in the areas of health care and welfare. Governments will force individuals to maintain and monitor their own health and wellness or be punished in a variety of mainly financial ways. This action will be strongly supported by the general population as it balances the selfish need for lower health care costs with the altruistic obligation that every citizen has not to be a burden to others. Two huge financial problems face most developed countries in the twenty-first century: pension costs and health care. The IMF recently calculated the cost of age-related spending for various countries up to 2050, and the numbers are astounding.

Again, I won't bore you with heavy statistics, but the current mind-blowing billion- and trillion-dollar stimulus packages that countries are throwing at the current economic crisis will add about 10 percent to the fiscal deficit of most developed countries. Age-related costs over the next 40 years will have 10 times the fiscal impact.

In countries where populations are declining, pension payment will be almost impossible to deliver when there are a disproportionate number of older people being supported by a declining group of younger, working-age taxpayers. This problem is becoming acute in Japan, Germany, and Italy, and will become so in various other countries within the next two decades. The worst-affected countries, despite having growing populations, will be Spain, by a long, long way, followed by the US, owing to excessive entitlement costs. If you live in either of these countries, buckle up for a rough ride over the next few years as taxes soar or entitlements are slashed. Or more likely both.

Health care costs are already a major issue for almost every developed country. Medical and health-related costs have risen inexorably, yet the more that is spent, the more that complaints seem to increase. Taxpayer funds are shoveled into the maw of the health dragon to prevent further fire being breathed on the unfortunate government in power. But it is all to no avail. No matter how much money is spent, it never seems to be sufficient to deliver a health service that meets the standard the population expects after all the taxes they pay.

Health care spending accounted for 15.2 percent of US GDP in 2003, and per-capita spending has more than doubled in a little over the past decade (see table 12.1).

Table 12.1 US health care spending per capita

Year	Spending in US dollars
1970	352
1980	1,072
1990	2,752
2003	5,771

Source: OECD

It is quite clear that neither the US nor any other country can keep increasing spending at this rate. However, the problem is being exacerbated by declining levels of fitness, a rapidly rising number of older people, hugely expensive equipment, outrageously priced drugs, and a shortage of trained staff. Health care reform is on the lips of governments everywhere as they extrapolate the impact of continued health cost increases on increasingly tight future budgets. The problem of finding a solution is further compounded by the interests of the huge number of people employed by the health services and related companies. Lobby groups abound, pressure groups proliferate, and vested interests are everywhere. Reform after reform is defeated. Technological solutions to increase efficiency are unsuccessful. Nothing seems to work when it is driven from the top down.

So government is realizing that the solution is to start at the bottom and work up. Literally at the bottom in some cases because obesity is one of the key health problems. It is clear that collaboration with users is again the key to success, just as it will be for companies in this time of collaboration and consensus. Government will need to work from the bottom up by working with individuals to help them maintain health and by designing medical services that the users want.

President Obama has developed a set of eight principles for health care reform, including one that insists it must "invest in prevention and wellness." Prevention is just as important as cure. In the past, medical services were geared to curing people who were sick and reacted to patient illness. However, the future of medicine will very much be related to the prediction and prevention of disease. An article in *Newsweek* magazine by Leroy Hood talks about P4 medicine: predictive, personalized, preventative, and participatory. Hood attributes this change in emphasis to powerful new technologies that are able to sample blood and analyze genes.

The UK is taking a similar tack, and is very much changing its medical approach to personalized and predictive medicine. However, there may well be a "sting in the tail" for individuals who do not take corrective action. The British government is already making plans to provide regular free screening to people at specific ages throughout their life to monitor the "big three" problems: obesity, diabetes, and high blood pressure. This will be an increasingly regular health check as people age, to detect medical problems at an early stage and solve them before they become endemic or incurable.

One of the tools they will use is produced by a company called Wellpoint, which manufactures an interactive health monitor. The monitor allows users to measure their own height, weight, body mass, and blood pressure. The user receives a printout of his or her last 10 visits, so they can see their progress—or lack of it. The data can be automatically transmitted to the person's central health files, so that his or her doctor can review the patient status, and recommend actions or prescribe medicines to prevent emerging medical problems. This type of equipment will be used to allow health self-monitoring by individuals, and the recording of their key data. Companies will offer a similar service to their employees, pharmacists to their customers, and doctors and hospitals to their patients. These voluntary tests will be suggested or recommended at first, until the process has been tested, and results can be observed. However, with any measure of success, these regular, monitored health tests will soon become mandatory.

An ounce of prevention is better, and a lot cheaper, than a pound of cure. So governments will soon mandate a regular series of tests at specific ages. Legislation will set the rules and every individual will have the responsibility to adhere to the measurement guidelines. Failure will result in some sort of financial penalty. Premiums on insurance policies will rise for nonconformists who cannot provide the results of their health checks, for example. People who consistently fall outside the health check guidelines on weight or blood pressure may find that their taxes increase to pay for a greater health service contribution. Whatever stick of enforcement is applied the result will be that the individual will be held much more responsible for their own health and welfare, instead of throwing the full burden on the state.

Companies will not be spared in this drive to apply pressure on individuals. The *New York Times* reported that "Congress is considering proposals to provide tax credits or other subsidies to employers who offer wellness programs that meet Federal criteria. In addition, law-makers said they would make it easier for employers to use financial rewards or penalties to promote healthy behavior among employees." A company will be able to reward employees for their high health standards, including having a better diet, taking more exercise, maintaining standard weight levels, and not smoking. The article continued that "employers could employ tax credits for programs that offer periodic screenings for health problems and counseling to help employees adopt healthier lifestyles." The ethical justification for this program is that "employees should be held responsible for voluntary actions that cause harm to others."

Welcome to the Age of Selfish Altruism. You must do what's best for yourself but ensure that no one is harmed by your actions.

Many corporations that have begun wellness programs have found that they can reduce health care costs and absenteeism, and improve productivity. Employers have provided the environment, the equipment, and financial incentives such as gift certificates, discounts, and subsidized food costs on healthy produce—and surcharges on less healthy foodstuffs and drinks. Government provides the legislation, business enables the programs, but the final responsibility for action is thrown back to the individual. This will be a defining characteristic of the twenty-first century.

The past century was shaped by the creation of the welfare state, a nanny state that took responsibility for its citizens. Pension plans, national health, and the government will take care of you. That twentieth-century model is financially unsustainable in this century. The state will still provide all the welfare benefits of the past century, but the cost and services delivered will vary by individual. Stay fit and you'll be rewarded. Be a blimp and expect to pay for the privilege. Human rights groups are already complaining and deeply oppose this type of new legislation, which impinges on an individual's freedom of action. They claim that people should not be discriminated against on the basis of their lifestyle. I'm afraid that they are like King Canute trying to hold back the tide. They have no chance of holding back this, or any other "new morality" legislation.

The new morality and selfish altruism of this new century, demands that every individual play a key role in the general welfare. We must sometimes make sacrifices for the general good. We must occasionally subsume our personal freedoms for the benefit of all.

Karl Marx must be smiling in his corner of heaven. We are seeing the creation of true social communism but without economic communism. This same ethical standard of not harming others has been used for the past couple of decades to restrict or punish smoking. If smokers' actions affect others they must pay the price. Where a smoker can light up has been curtailed dramatically, especially since the start of this century, with total smoking bans in offices, restaurants, bars, and public areas. The additional burden that smokers place upon the health services has been paid for through huge taxes on cigarettes, and the additional premium that smokers pay for insurance. This same philosophy will be applied to the general population in the effort to encourage healthy lifestyles and identify any potential illnesses early. This will be the primary method of health care "reform," and the most direct way to address the problem. All other solutions may be like rearranging the chairs on the Titanic. We need to melt the iceberg, not reduce the cost of services on the ship.

Governments will therefore soon enforce upon all their citizens what companies are now being empowered to do with their employees.

Mandatory health checks and monitoring will soon become a condition of participation in free health services in the future. Failure to adhere to the medical screenings and the action demanded will result in higher personal taxes to pay for the potential impact on the health service. Screening for diseases will start at birth, or even in the womb to take immediate corrective action and prevent later illness. Genetic changes early in life will become a key feature of health care to counteract hereditary diseases or susceptibility to various illnesses. Inoculations and other disease-prevention activity will be a feature of early life, as they are now. But it will be mandatory.

Screening for obesity, diabetes, and high blood pressure will begin early, and continue throughout everyone's lives at increasingly frequent intervals with age. Just as a car has to be serviced at certain mileage points, humans will have the same demands. At various ages, certain tests will be mandated. Everyone will receive instructions to undergo specific tests at every key age throughout their lives. Failure to undergo the screening in the time frame demanded, will result in personal taxes on the individual being increased, and they will face other financial penalties. Anyone who doesn't adhere to the health check regime will suffer a significant personal impact through higher taxes, loss of insurance coverage, removal of certain benefits, and more difficult commercial transactions such as home mortgages. All of us alive in the twenty-first century will pay for failure to stay healthy and be checked regularly.

It may even reach the stage of performance monitoring equipment being placed on people who fail key health tests to ensure that they undertake the behavioral changes mandated. Prisoners are released on parole with a transmitter locked around their ankle so that their movement can be monitored. A similar system could well be used to ensure that obese people exercise regularly, or are barred from fast food outlets. It may sound far-fetched, but either draconian action needs to be taken or health care systems will implode or become completely unaffordable. Health care will be taken just as seriously as environmental responsibility, and nonparticipation will not be an option. Already an iPhone application can measure heart rate and transmit the data for analysis, and other sensors can measure caloric burn rate. Soon, personal devices will direct and monitor health performance, transmit the data, and change your exercise regimen accordingly.

All this enforced action will put considerable strain on individuals and their right to selfishly live as they please. However the government's actions will be with the common consent of the people, who believe that no one has the right to affect others adversely. "We" will accept, and even demand, these behavioral impositions for the common good. This is the new morality and Age of Selfish Altruism.

> *A man too busy to take care of his health is like a mechanic too busy to take care of his tools.*
> —Spanish proverb

The Twenty-First-Century Dilemma

Selfish altruism is a paradox. Almost every decision has to be weighed up in one's mind as a balance between what *I* want, and what *we* believe is the "right thing to do." Whenever we make a decision, no matter how large or small, we are always making "tradeoffs" in our mind. This is especially true when we are buying a product or service. Traditional marketing theory has been based on us being rational human beings who make sensible decisions. The psychological decision-making process in most marketing textbooks is usually expressed as a hierarchical pyramid or an onion in which the layers are gradually peeled away to reach the core reasons for purchase and loyalty. We also read a lot about left-brain versus right-brain people: the rational versus the emotional; logical versus creative; intuitive versus experiential.

However, this distinction is not clear cut: "A clear distinction between emotional and rational is not possible. The left and the right part of the brain are strongly connected in our decision making. You can compare it to a concert," said Antonio Rosa Damasio, a behavioral neurologist and neuroscientist.

Professor Wilhelm Salber has developed a theory in which he views decision making as a holistic process within an overall framework that he calls "morphology." Morphological psychology says that decisions are not driven by one single desire, but are a result of mental negotiation as the mind balances different motivations. Salber has identified three "tensions," which come into play when we have to make a decision:

- stability and innovation
- relationship and practical value
- vision and competence.

The first concerns our desire to stick with what we know, when it feels comfortable for us, but at the same time to experience the new. The second pits our affection, what we like, against what we need, what works. The third contrasts our dreams with our ability to realize them.

When looked at from a morphological perspective, selfish altruism makes perfect sense. Morphological research shows us that everyday activities are not driven by just one core motivation, but are a result of negotiating a broad range of motivations. Our conscious and subconscious combine around these three fundamental "tensions." The mental "negotiation" we go through helps us find common ground between our rational conscious brain, and our unconscious psychological needs. That's why the products and brands we buy don't simply serve the functional purpose for which they seem to be made, but also satisfy a range of emotional needs. As we have noted, whereas the twentieth century was all about self-esteem, status, and image, the twenty-first century combines that selfish rationale with the altruistic desire to do the right thing and the desire for self-actualization. The balance between selfishness and altruism will lead to tradeoffs and contradictions that marketers will need to recognize and reflect.

Table 12.2 shows some of the key dichotomies that we will struggle with in the Age of Selfish Altruism.

Table 12.2 Dichotomies of the Age of Selfish Altruism

Dichotomy	Outcomes
More vs. less	We will have a willingness to pay more, but a desire to buy, and own, less. Although possessions will always raise our self-esteem, and show status and achievements, we are realizing that values and relationships are equally or much more important. So when we buy nowadays, we have to balance our need for self-esteem with our aspiration for self-actualization.
Big vs. small	We will have the desire to live better, but to consume less. The twenty-first century will see us wanting a healthier, higher-quality, more environmentally considerate lifestyle, but having to accept smaller spaces, tinier portions, lower consumption, and a far less ostentatious lifestyle.
Science vs. morality	We will want all the benefits of scientific advancement, but we will have a greater moral awareness and concern over the direction it takes. We will realize the benefits of our ability to adapt genes, clone the natural world and ourselves, and build robots, but we will be wary of the ethical downsides.

(continued)

Table 12.2 (*Continued*)

Dichotomy	Outcomes
Real ID vs. real me	We will accept less individualism in the "real" world, but revel in the greater individualism of the online world. The paradox is between what I want to reveal about myself versus the identity systems that are demanded of me. Benefits have to be really significant before people provide personal data that they fear could be used or abused.
Community vs. clan	We will feel a greater sense of global community, yet we will be ever more committed to our families. As the online world broadens our networks and brings us in touch with wider communities, we will focus all the more on our narrower "clan."
Success vs. happiness	We will still strive to be successful, but our idea of what success is will change. The pursuit of happiness will triumph over the pursuit of money.
Self vs. altruism	We will look after ourselves, as we always have, but we will want to look after others too. This is the most important balancing act of the twenty-first century.

Are We Already in the Age of Selfish Altruism?

How many of these balancing acts already exist in your mind and in your life? Are you still very much focused on the consumerism associated with self-esteem, or are you becoming a postconsumer, searching for more meaning, morality, and self-actualization? Are you already in the Age of Selfish Altruism?

The new tensions that we have to balance in our minds and the moral quandaries we increasingly face are a result of a big shift in our values and ethics. Some ethical issues you will feel very strongly about, while others will be less important to you. How you personally balance "self" versus "society" could be different from the way that your friends do. The way that you define "me" versus "we" may also differ from others.

However, every one of us is going to be faced with this same mental and behavioral balancing act in this Age of Selfish Altruism.

This book may only have chronicled what is already emerging in your mind, and increasingly in that of millions of others. Or even billions of others. So listen to yourself, and be guided by the new twenty-first-century values and morality that you are creating. Don't be embarrassed by what you feel.

If you're a career-oriented person, think about how to apply the important elements of the Age of Selfish Altruism to your business. You should seek to help your company position itself for this century and shape the way it does business to meet the new ethics and morals of your customers. This will require an understanding and careful monitoring of changes in their attitudes and behavior. Offer your company a new vision for the future and ensure that it is not operating on an old twentieth-century business model.

What you need to keep in mind, in both your personal and business life, is that as the world shifts toward greater self-actualization it will become a key driver of everyone's behavior. A new postconsumer is emerging as people begin to ask questions about what they are buying and why. Sales volumes may therefore not simply keep increasing, and managing decline may be necessary in many markets, as quality trumps quantity, and maturing populations change their purchase habits. Value and values will become as important as price and function, so it will be critical to stay in touch with consumers and their changing hierarchy of needs.

Get prepared for government to become much more intrusive in business life. "You can't fight City Hall," so look for ways to work with policymakers to help them understand that a carrot can often achieve much better results than a stick. Government will also become a lot more dictatorial in your personal life, but this will be because you asked for it! So get used to living with new rules and lifestyle restrictions.

Whatever your aspirations and goals, you are now in a new century that will be very different from the last one. The speed of technological change and scientific advancement will be astounding, so defining and maintaining the highest standards of ethics and morals will be of the greatest importance to future human life. The ability of everyone to communicate and build consensus will be a marvelous tool that will give you the ability to influence millions of others, and to join them in a drive to "do what's right." You will be influenced by many people, and sometimes face unexpected challenges in your business or personal life. So it is most important that you find your own moral and ethical balance which can act as bedrock for your opinions and actions.

Only when you find that special balance between selfishness and altruism will you be able to lead a much more fulfilling, enjoyable and happier life. And if you can save the planet at the same time, what could be better?

Welcome to the Age of Selfish Altruism.

Index